THE NEW LAW BUSINESS MODEL

THE
NEW LAW
BUSINESS
MODEL
REVEALED

BUILD A LUCRATIVE LAW PRACTICE
THAT YOU (AND YOUR CLIENTS) **LOVE**

ALI KATZ

LIONCREST

PUBLISHING

THE NEW LAW BUSINESS MODEL

Build a Lucrative Law Practice That You (and Your Clients) Love

ISBN   978-1-5445-0465-0 *Paperback*

      978-1-5445-0466-7 *Ebook*

      978-1-5445-0467-4 *Audiobook*

To Kaia, Noah, and Todd: Without the three of you, I never would have discovered the traditional law practice model was broken—nor would I have had the motivation to create the new law business model that has enriched our lives immeasurably. I love you forever and ever and ever.

CONTENTS

INTRODUCTION

If you're reading this book, I'm going to go out on a limb and assume you're a lawyer, or on your way to becoming a lawyer. But you've begun to notice (or maybe have known for a very long time) that something is not right, and this *being a lawyer* business doesn't seem to be quite what you'd imagined.

You went to law school with a dream of making a great living while making a real difference in people's lives— maybe even in the world. In the process, you were going to be able to have a family or hobbies, and maybe even become a respected, valued, and appreciated member of your community. All that, plus you would provide a great life for yourself and your family.

This dream was so powerful, and you believed in it so much, that you were willing to work hard and make sacrifices to see it happen. You probably even took on significant student loan debt to do it.

That was the promise, right?

Now it's beginning to dawn on you that not only can you not have it all, but you can't seem to have *any* of it.

Whether you're just starting out or you've been in practice twenty-five years or more, chances are you're still working crazy hours—and *still* not making (or keeping) the kind of money you expected. And, definitely not making the impact you'd hoped for.

You may spend your days dealing with antagonistic opposing counsel, and it's turning you into an angry, agitated person—not only in the office, but at home.

Overworked and underappreciated, you're finding it hard to empathize with your clients, and even harder to find the patience to deal with your own family. As you've started to think through all of this, perhaps you even fear that you've lost some of your humanity.

You are not the person you once were, or the person you set out to be.

The worst part of it is that your interests aren't even aligned with your clients' interests. Not really. Instead of getting paid to resolve conflict, you may actually make your living by escalating it.

Along with your depressing home life and crushed vision of your career, you're lost in a morass of technology that you either can't figure out (or that you are scared you have to compete with), dropping your fees lower and lower along the way.

It's affecting your health. It's affecting your sleep. It's affecting the way you feel about your profession, and yourself.

This is *not* what you signed up for, and you're starting to wonder if going to law school was a huge mistake.

If this sounds like you, keep reading. I have good news for you.

Fantastic news.

The best news possible.

THE GOOD NEWS

This is *not* the time to be rethinking your career. Right now, you are in exactly the right place at exactly the right time to leverage the most valuable asset you could possibly have: your law degree.

Going to law school was not a mistake. In fact, getting your law degree was the very *best* thing you ever could have done. You just need to know how to use it in a new way, and that's what I'm going to teach you in this book.

Just like you, I went to law school with a vision and a dream of making a difference in my clients' lives while having a great family life. Early on, though, I realized the traditional, transactional way of running a law practice—where you must constantly seek the next new client to sustain an endless string of one-off transactions—didn't allow for that. I was shocked to discover what the practice of law was actually like. My dream wasn't just impractical, it seemed so *impossible* that I considered giving up law altogether.

Rather than leaving the law, though, I decided to figure out how I could be the kind of lawyer I wanted to be, with a law practice I loved, while having a great life, and experiencing the deep meaning and fulfillment that would come from using my law degree to truly serve clients in a meaningful way. It took me more than ten years and hundreds of thousands of dollars to put all the pieces together.

Many times, I wanted to give up. I questioned what the heck I was doing and why. I remember walking down the hall of my office, thinking to myself, Alexis, why are you doing this? Why are you risking it all? You're making massive investments of time and money in your practice with no guarantees that you'll *ever* figure this out!

Do you know how I kept going and encouraged myself? With thoughts of *you*. I knew I wasn't the only one who longed for a law practice model that really worked. I knew others like me were out there and just as fed up as I was with the traditional law practice model.

So, whenever I questioned what I was doing or the massive investments I was making in creating something new, I'd say to myself, "You're not just doing this for yourself, Alexis, or even just for your family. You're doing it for every other lawyer out there who feels the same way you do, and who needs someone to show them a way out. Everything you do right now will help those lawyers realize their own dreams. And they won't have to reinvent the wheel to get there because of what you're doing now. *Keep going.*" And I did.

I remember the moment it *really* hit me that the traditional law practice model wasn't just a bad fit for idealistic lawyers like me, but that it was completely and irrevocably broken. You'd think I would have figured this out sooner—*before* I'd invested years of my life and hundreds of thousands of dollars designing a practice I love—but I hadn't.

That lightbulb moment came much later, and it hit me like a ton of bricks.

A few years after I created what is now the *New Law Business Model*, I was hosting a live event. I asked each of the lawyers why they were there. What was it about their current situation that made them want to look for another way to practice law?

Richard, a litigator, stood up and told us about a day when he had been filing interrogatories for a case. He calculated the day they would be due and realized that with his filing, he would be ruining opposing counsel's Christmas. He began to pump his fist in the air in celebration.

Mid-fist-pump, Richard realized he had become someone who was celebrating ruining another human being's holiday. Richard had become someone he never imagined.

In that moment, Richard was suddenly aware that this same attitude was permeating not just his professional life, but his personal life. At work and at home, Richard had become an angry, combative human.

Shortly after that, Richard joined us to learn the *New Law Business Model*, so he could return to the reason he went to law school in the first place, and take back his humanity.

I've thought about Richard often over the years, especially in times of uncertainty, when I've found myself wondering, *Do I really want to devote my life to serving lawyers? If so, why?*

I know I wasn't put on this planet just to help lawyers make more money. But each time I think about Richard, I remember this: it's about so much more than that.

Yes, the lawyers who learn and apply the *New Law Business Model* make more money. But far more importantly, they take back their lives and their humanity. They become better parents, better business owners, and better neighbors. And more than ever, we need that right now.

IS THE *NEW LAW BUSINESS MODEL* FOR YOU?

I wrote this book for all of the lawyers who are unhappy in their old-school traditional transactional law practices—sick and tired of billing by-the-hour or one-off transactions that leave no room for building a meaningful life or practice.

And if you're a hard-core litigator and becoming someone you're not proud of, like Richard was, then this book is for you, too.

This book is for lawyers struggling to keep up with all the new technologies, and possibly facing major unemployment from online disruptors like WillsandTrusts, LegalZoom, and RocketLawyer, among the many online or automated legal service sites. We know they are a far cry from real attorneys, and yet you may still find yourself competing with them in a race to the bottom on price and services.

But here's the thing: none of that is the highest and best use of your law degree. With the *New Law Business Model*, your law degree and the right practice model, you have the knowledge, skills, and, most importantly, the heart and soul necessary to make a real impact in your clients' lives. You'll gain complete control over your schedule and your income, while delivering a truly meaningful service to clients who are more than willing—even happy and grateful—to pay for it.

I've now trained thousands of lawyers in the *New Law Business Model,* and they have seen the results: previously unhappy, unfulfilled, overworked lawyers are now building high six- and seven-figure law practices; making a significantly positive difference in the lives of their clients and in their communities. And they're having fun doing it.

I know it may sound too good to be true, but it's not. By the time you are done reading this book, you will have a vision of your life and law practice that's so inspiring, you'll do whatever it takes to make that vision a reality.

You will not have to take the big risks I took because I've done the heavy lifting of trial and error for you (and trust me, there were lots and lots of errors). I've built the systems you need to break free from long hours and miserable work in a broken law business model.

The lawyers who have implemented the *New Law Business*

Model have built financially sustainable, thriving law practices that they are proud of, that make them excited to go into the office (or work from home), *and* that give them plenty of time for family, travel, hobbies, or volunteer work on the side.

You can make the switch to the *New Law Business Model* too, and it's not as hard as you think.

I promise, it will be much harder to spend the next twenty or thirty years of your life serving clients who (perhaps understandably) don't appreciate you—and liking yourself even less than they do—than it will be to put in six to eighteen months learning a better way.

If you're thinking you're too new to law or have been practicing it so long that it's too late to make a change, I have more good news: the *New Law Business Model* works for any lawyer at any stage of their career. If you are willing to invest time, energy, attention, and money (we call these your TEAM resources) in truly creating a life and law practice you love, your investment *will* pay off.

If you're just coming out of law school, there's no transition required. You can start your practice from scratch the right way, right from the beginning. You may see money as the greatest obstacle, but the fact is that if you've just graduated you *have* time, which is much more valuable than money.

Time is a nonrenewable asset, whereas money is infinitely renewable when you know how to deliver a service that people need. And your law degree, when used well, is perfect for that!

Litigators transitioning to *The New Law Business Model* will have to put in place some clear boundaries to find the time. Currently, you're at the whim of the court and opposing counsel—which should be enough, in itself, to motivate you to make the switch. With the *New Law Business Model*, all of that stops. You can do this, and I'll provide you with a time-blocking and calendaring system that will make it easier than you think.

If you're currently doing trusts and estate work or corporate, commercial, or business work the traditional way (using the transactional model), then you already have the legal foundation in place to make the switch to the *New Law Business Model* fairly quickly. You *will* have to learn how to overcome the bad habits you've learned, though, such as taking on too many clients because you're not charging enough for your services.

Once you've committed to learning this new model and have made the switch, you will have to get comfortable with working fewer hours and making more money.

Consider what your life would look like if you loved your law practice.

Imagine it's two years from now. Who are you? What does your life look like? Is it the same as it is right now? Probably not.

So the question is: are you going to keep doing what you're doing the way you're doing it, or are you willing to invest the time, energy, attention, and money to create something entirely new? If your vision of the future calls for some radical changes, this book will guide you through them, all the way to the life you've been dreaming of.

You went to law school—or you're there right now—to make a difference in your clients' lives. You envisioned being a trusted advisor and counselor for your clients. Maybe even a teacher of the law.

It's time to live up to all those promises you made to yourself. It's time to take back your heart, your home life, your income, your humanity, and your dream of creating better communities.

This is the *New Law Business Model*. I designed it, I use it, and I've taught it to thousands of other lawyers. It works.

TOO GOOD TO BE TRUE?

This all sounds good, maybe too good, you're probably thinking. *So what's the catch? Why do* you *want to help* me? If you aren't thinking that right now, you should be. You're a lawyer, and those are the kinds of questions that are always running through our minds, right?

I don't want you to read the whole book while wondering what my hidden agenda is, or if I'm trying to sell you something. So, here's my agenda, right out on the table for you. I'm not going to hide it.

> I want to support you in your transition from a life and law practice model that isn't working for you to one that will allow you to have a life and law practice that you truly love. If you decide to make that transition by serving families and/ or small business owners as a counselor and trusted advisor, then I want you to use the resources I've created, so you don't have to reinvent the wheel. You don't have to go through the extreme trial and error or massive investment that I did, because I've already done it for you.

You may *still* be skeptical, and that makes sense. Lawyers are naturally skeptical. We're bombarded with people trying to sell us marketing solutions. Many of you may have already taken a shot at investing in marketing or lead generation programs that didn't work. "Fool me once..." I get it. No one likes to be made a fool, and lawyers—with our intelligence, education, *and* skepticism—get really ticked off when someone screws us over. We are *trained* to see through the crap. It's what we *do*.

Don't let go of that healthy skepticism. It's probably served you well, and without it, you wouldn't be you, and you probably wouldn't be a very good lawyer. But be willing to embrace the unknown, too, because that's what's necessary to become an entrepreneur.

If you can put aside enough of your skepticism to really take a look at the process and the results I've created, I can shift your life. Your law degree will become your most valuable asset, not just financially, but as a tool to help you use your time, energy, and creative genius in a way that's truly meaningful for you, your family, and the clients you serve.

Okay, maybe I *am* trying to sell you something. I'm selling you on the life and law practice you actually want. I'm selling you on the possibility of making that happen more efficiently, effectively, and affordably than if you tried to create it on your own.

I hear your lawyer-mind wondering, *But what do you* really *want from me?* I want you to take what I'm about to share with you in this book and use it to take control over your schedule and your income stream, and to make a real difference in your clients' lives by supporting them to stay out of court and out of conflict. Whether you go it on your own or with the full support of one of my *New Law Business Model* training programs, there's one thing I can pretty much guarantee: once you've tried practicing law the *NLBM* way, you'll never, ever want to go back to the way it was. And you'll never have to.

But first, let's back up. Before I can show you what's possible for you and your law practice, I need to tell you how this all started.

PART ONE

—

FOUNDATIONS

CHAPTER ONE

MY PRACTICE TRANSFORMATION

"When the student is ready, the teacher appears."

—UNKNOWN

I had my first brush with the law—or rather, my first brush with the traditional, transactional law business model—before I actually started practicing law. It wasn't good, and at the time, I couldn't understand it. Looking back, the experience should have been my first clue that there was something horribly wrong with the traditional law business model. Here's how it all played out.

My father-in-law died just after I had graduated law school, while I was still at my post-law-school clerkship. Before he died, he had spent $3,000 on an estate plan. He did so *specifically* to keep his family from having to deal with the probate court after his death, and *specifically* to keep us from having to deal with his ex-wife. So, you can imagine how confusing it was when, after he died, we were left dealing with the probate court *and* his ex-wife.

You see, while my father-in-law had put in place an estate plan, thinking everything was taken care of, that plan had never been updated, and his assets weren't owned in the right way to keep us out of court or from having to deal with his ex-wife after he died. And, as crazy as this may seem, more than twenty years later, there are STILL assets of my father-in-law stuck in Florida's Department of Unclaimed Property.

My father-in-law had paid $3,000 for a set of documents that he didn't even understand, signed them, taken them home, put them on a shelf, and never looked at them again, thinking he had done what he needed to do to take care of the people he loved. But he hadn't. And now we were going to have to pay his lawyer more money to clean up the mess.

I thought for sure the lawyer who had served my father-in-law must have committed malpractice. But very shortly after, I went to work at one of the best law firms in the country as an associate in the estate planning group, and discovered it wasn't malpractice at all—this was *common* practice.

This was how lawyers—even those at the best law firms in the country—did estate planning. *What was going on?*

MALPRACTICE OR COMMON PRACTICE?

To say I was alarmed is an understatement. This was a major problem, and I was determined to figure it out. I began interviewing estate planning lawyers across the country.

Shockingly, every lawyer I spoke to was putting in place estate plans the exact same way that my father-in-law's lawyer had. Their clients were paying these transactional lawyers—who made a living by churning through as many clients as possible, as quickly as possible—for wills, trusts, or powers of attorney that they thought would keep their family out of court. The clients took those documents home and filed them away in a drawer or on a bookshelf, checked "estate planning" off their to-do list, and never looked at them again—only for the family to find out (when it was too late) that those documents had never been updated and didn't actually work.

So, the family, aghast, dismayed, and still reeling from the loss of their loved one, would return to the lawyer. They would ask what assets their now incapacitated or deceased family member had, but the lawyer wouldn't know. She hadn't inventoried the assets in the first place, the documents weren't updated over time, and there was no clear process for transferring the assets to the family without unnecessary conflict and expensive, wasted hours in court. This isn't just a problem in estate planning; it's *common practice* in all sorts of transactional practice areas, including legal work done for business owners.

Another common example: a pair of new business owners go to a lawyer to set up their business. They sign a bunch of documents and figure they're legally golden.

Sometime down the line, there's a dispute between the business partners, or they get sued, or one wants to sell her shares in a hurry—and guess what? The proper agreements aren't in place. The shares were never issued. The business was incorporated, but the owners never received the ongoing support to ensure that it was set up to thrive with the right legal structure, insurance net, financial plan, or tax foundations.

If this is how *you* practice, it's not your fault. It's how it's done. It's how we've been taught (or *not* taught, really).

Maybe you want to do a better job for your clients, instead of feeling like a human version of LegalZoom. You are, after all, a human being, and you want to actually make a difference in your clients' lives. But no one ever taught you how to do that, as a lawyer.

The transactional law practice model teaches us how to put in place documents for our clients as quickly as possible, so we can then move on to the next new client, and the next new client after that. As a result, you probably know you are leaving your clients with documents they don't really understand and will rarely look at again, if ever. And in most cases, their assets aren't inventoried and aren't owned in the right way to actually achieve their objectives and keep their family (or their business) out of court and out of conflict. These are the consequences of all this legal work that doesn't really work.

Again, I didn't figure this out overnight. After the debacle with my father-in-law's estate, I finished law school, started a family, and fell into the traditional, transactional model of practicing law myself. It didn't feel good, though.

But, what other choice did I have?

COMMITMENT PRECEDES CLARITY

In 2002, I was working hard in the corporate tax and estate planning department of one of the best law firms in the country, providing for my family and trying to be the lawyer I thought I had been trained to be, yet I was terribly unhappy. I didn't go to law school to help big corporations pay fewer taxes, to help rich people get richer. I went to law school to make a real difference in people's lives, and I just couldn't see how that was happening doing high-end corporate tax work.

I had thought I'd be helping *people*, not just corporations.

My daily commute to the law firm in L.A. was an hour each

way, and during one of those long drives, I made a decision and a commitment: I would build my own book of business serving families and small business owners, inside the BigLaw firm.

I talked to the firm, and they gave me the reluctant okay to move forward with creating my own client base. This was very unusual for a BigLaw firm, and I'll always be grateful that they let me try to build my own book of business as a second-year associate.

I had no idea how I was going to do it, but I knew it was vitally important for me to figure it out. I was committed to finding a way to love my life and law practice, even though I lacked clarity about how that would happen or what it would look like.

It was that commitment that would pull me through to discover my next steps, and I encourage you to make your own commitment to a life and law practice you love, now.

When you make a commitment (even without knowing how you'll do it or what it will look like), clarity follows, and that's what happened for me, repeatedly.

Once I'd made the firm decision to build my own book of business at the BigLaw firm, my first action was to attend a "women in business" event at my local chamber of commerce, hoping to meet some new clients.

I took out a business-card-sized ad in the brochure for the event, saying something like, "Alexis Martin Neely—Wills, Trusts, Estates." (Alexis Martin Neely was my name at the time.) I was so excited to be putting myself out there for the first time. Of course, I knew nothing about marketing and the ad was a total waste of money, but I was naïve and eager.

And, when the student is ready, the teacher appears.

At the event, there was a speaker giving a presentation on branding, and to tell you the truth, I did not hear a word she said about branding. What I did hear was that she had her own business. She worked from home and made her own schedule. She was there when her son came home from school. She loved her job, and her clients loved her.

As I listened to her talk, my heart began to light up. I had never heard anything like what she was describing. Today, of course, it's commonplace to hear about women working from home in fulfilling careers, but back then it was still a novel idea. And as I heard her talk about her life and business, I thought to myself, *Wow, I want that. How can I have that for myself?*

And a mantra I would repeat over the years as I saw other men and women creating what I wanted in my own life was born: *If she can do it, I can do it. If he can do it, I can do it.*

I encourage you to adopt this mantra for yourself. Use it if you like what you see out there, instead of letting envy—or excuses about why successful entrepreneurs are different from you—stop you. Know that this mantra is pointing you toward what you want, that you can do it too.

After the event, I decided to buy the speaker's book, praying it would have some answers about how I could create a life I loved, just like she had.

And I found the answers I was seeking. In the acknowledgment's section of the book was the name of the speaker's business coach. Oh, a coach, I thought. I guess I could hire a coach. But that's weird. And probably a waste of money.

Seventeen years ago, coaching was not as popular as it is today. It was still pretty *out there*, and I already felt as if I didn't fit in at the BigLaw firm as it was. Plus, I was highly resistant to spending any money on myself. I had never done it before, didn't think I could afford it, and my mind was screaming at me: *You don't need no stinking coach. There's no way she's as smart as you. You graduated first in your class from Georgetown Law. You don't need to spend money on a coach, Ali!*

Thankfully, I didn't listen to those thoughts, because if I had, I'd probably still be working in BigLaw, by now as an "of counsel" attorney, working full-time hours and getting paid part time, with very little to no respect for my work.

Fortunately, I was able to see that the part of my mind that didn't want me to pursue hiring a coach was scared, and trying to keep me safe. And I was able to thank that part and remind it that the speaker I had seen had a great life and career, and had written a book, and *she* had a coach. Maybe there was something to this coaching stuff.

I put my ego aside, tracked down the coach, and called her.

She was in Atlanta, but she said she could coach me by phone and email for $350 a month.

Three hundred and fifty dollars a month? At the time it seemed absurd. Even though I was making $185,000 a year, my paycheck was gone after the mortgage payment, car payments, insurance, student loans, taxes, 401(k) plans, gas for the car, and food and clothing. I was supporting my stay-at-home husband and our child. Spending anything on myself wasn't even a consideration.

Looking back, I have to laugh at how little I knew about money. Today, I invest thousands of dollars a month on coaching support, and that investment pays off consistently.

But back then, I was terrified to invest in myself, even though I was desperate for a change.

Despite my fear, I did it anyway.

And I am so thankful I did. It changed everything.

In our first session, my coach started asking me odd questions: *When was the last time you went to the dentist? When was your last pedicure? What about a haircut? And, have you been to the gym lately?*

This was ridiculous, and I was pissed. Here I had come up with (what was to me) a bunch of money—though with a huge amount of fear around it—and this woman was quizzing me about my personal hygiene.

"Hey," I said, "I'm not paying you to talk about my toenails. I'm a busy lawyer, and I don't have the time or the money for pedicures. I want you to teach me how to love my job the way that the author you coached loves her job."

Well, my coach must have heard this before, because she was prepared for it. She wasn't defensive at all, but spoke with confidence and certainty.

She said, "Until you are taking care of yourself, you're not going to love anything you do."

Hmmm, okay, take care of myself. I wonder what that even means? I thought. Then: I still don't believe her, but whatever. Let's see where this goes. I'll do what she says.

I made an appointment to see a dentist, got my first pedicure, and got my hair cut at a salon.

I joined a gym and started getting up an hour earlier to work out every morning. An unexpected perk was that by leaving the house that early, I avoided the usual rush hour traffic. I'd creep out of bed at the crack of dawn, leave my husband and baby girl sleeping, and enjoy the sunrise coming up over the freeway on my way to the gym.

Before I could find my love of being a lawyer, I had to find myself.

I'm telling you all this for a reason. **If you're not taking care of yourself, you need to start doing that—right now. It might seem like a waste of time and money, but trust me, you need to care for yourself before you can care about anything else, like your clients or your business, or even your family.** And it's very likely you never learned how. I certainly hadn't. Still, I don't think it really even sank in for me how important this was until a near-death experience woke me up.

TRANSFORMING THE VOICE

Driving east on the I-10 in L.A. one morning in my Volkswagen GTI, I was enjoying the light, pre-rush-hour traffic as I watched the sun rise over the freeway.

Suddenly, the car ahead of me swerved, and a huge roll of carpet appeared in the middle of the road, right in the path of my car.

I could hit the carpet head-on or swerve around it like the car in front of me had. I swerved, and the next thing I knew, I was spinning across the highway, seemingly out of control. A voice boomed in my head, *"Turn into the skid! Turn into the skid!"* I did just that, and my car came to a screeching halt against the center median, facing in the wrong direction.

As I got out to assess the damage, the voice yelled at me again, *"Get back in the car and move—now!"*

I jumped back into my car. Within seconds, another car spun across the freeway and slammed, head-first, into the median—exactly where I had been standing seconds before.

Shaken, I realized that the voice had saved me—twice. I was alive because the voice in my head had told me exactly what to do, and I had followed its direction.

In that moment, I realized that voice had been with me my whole life, but it had never seemed very helpful before. In the past, the voice had seemed to be constantly harassing me, *"You're not good enough. You don't fit in. What's wrong with you? Why can't you just be happy? No one likes you. You're so dumb—why are you such an idiot?"* Up until that day.

Now, though, the tone of the voice had changed. The voice had saved my life. The voice had changed because *I* had changed.

The pedicures, haircuts, dental work, and exercise had paid off, just as my coach had said they would! I was taking care of myself, and my inner voice reflected that. No longer was it harassing me with put-downs and criticism. For the first time in my life, my inner voice had my back; it said, "*I've got you, I'm here and I'm going to keep you safe. I'm going to keep you alive.*"

I began to listen to my inner voice more closely after that. And I began to hear it encouraging me to consider that maybe life was too short to keep working at a job I didn't love, even if millions of other lawyers and law students would kill for that job.

Maybe I could create a law practice that would support the life I really wanted *and* allow me to make a real difference in my clients' lives *and* make a great living too. Maybe...

It took a near-death experience for me to realize that life is too short to hate your job and too unpredictable to put off doing something about it. I had to fix my life and career trajectory—*now*, not later.

I couldn't waste anymore time doing work I didn't believe

in and living a life I didn't love. And building my own book of business inside the BigLaw firm was not going to save me.

I thought about my options; and staying in a life and law practice that I hated for the next thirty to fifty years was *not* one of them. I could quit the law, but I knew that if I did, the question would gnaw at me: what if I had tried to build a law practice that I loved and that my clients loved?

I wanted to work differently. I wanted to use my law degree to make a difference and a great living and be able to have a *life*. And I was going to figure it out—whatever "it" was— come hell or high water.

MAKING THE LEAP

I made a new commitment to myself that day: before I turned thirty, I would give up my job at the BigLaw firm and start my own law practice.

In March 2003, at twenty-nine years old, my second child was born—while I was in labor *and* on phone calls throughout the day with the senior partner I worked for at the BigLaw firm. That was when I decided quitting-day may be coming sooner than I'd thought.

I never went back after my maternity leave. Instead, I did the most terrifying (at the time) thing in the world.

With a brand-new baby, a four-year-old, and my husband staying at home to take care of them (read: no secondary income), I quit my $185,000 a year-plus-benefits and a 401(k), prestigious, BigLaw firm job.

The next thing I did was reach out to a lawyer who had been doing estate and business work for families in my community of Torrance, California, for twenty-five years. I asked if he would trade me space in his high-rise building in exchange for twenty hours a week of my legal services. He agreed, saving me $2,000 a month in rent. The space was much smaller than my old office, but with no savings in the bank, it was a saving grace. I bought some used furniture and picked up a new laptop on credit. But beyond a website and a computer, I had little understanding of what I would need to start my practice.

Let me be clear here: I was *not* excited to be a business owner.

I hadn't invested years of my life and more than $100,000 in student loans because I was a gambler or a risk-taker. I'd made those choices because I believed I was betting on a sure thing: a career that would equate to a steady income and a job for life.

But, turning that sure thing into a job and life I actually loved meant I needed to start my own business.

I was both terrified and exhilarated, and some part of me even thought it would be easy. I would go out and talk to the other parents in my community about estate planning, then they would call me, hire me, and I would easily get four or so clients a month at $2,500 each, and that would be enough.

I figured that my old paycheck—after taxes and insurance and retirement and all that—was less than $10,000 per month. So, if I made $10,000 per month in my own practice I'd be rolling in the dough.

Right.

If you've been working on your own for any amount of time, you know what a false dream that is. No matter how good of a lawyer you are, or how good what you offer is, people are procrastinators by nature. Especially when it comes to estate planning. I mean, who wants to think about death, right?

And, at the time, I didn't realize that businesses cost real money to run. If I brought in $10,000 a month, I would only be able to keep a fraction of that *unless* I wanted to spend all my days and nights doing assistant-level tasks like answering my phones, following up on client leads, rescheduling appointments, sending (and trying to collect on) invoices, responding to a million emails, and on and on.

Oh, there was so much to learn.

I didn't know where the resources would come from, and I didn't have any money in the bank—and when I say, "didn't have any money in the bank," I mean zero, zilch, nada. I couldn't even afford my own office, after all.

I spent my days networking and my weekends and evenings giving talks in my community to people who would thank me for the great information, tell me they were going to call me, and then disappear forever.

I didn't know what I was going to do. This was going to be nowhere near as simple as I'd thought. I was really scared.

Fortunately, I had some spillover work that had come with me from the BigLaw firm, and that kept me going for a while. But I knew I needed to figure something out, and *fast*, if I wanted to be able to keep working for myself and not have to take another BigLaw job.

Or end up like the guys I saw working at the law firm I shared space with.

It was crazy. I saw them working all hours of the day and night—weekends, too, even. And not because management was making them do it (they *were* the management!), but because they didn't seem to know a better way. There were no systems in place for ensuring a steady stream of clients, and no processes for automating the tedious work that cluttered their schedules. Every time a new client would come in, they would scramble to reinvent the wheel to serve them. In between clients, they seemed to waste a lot of time worrying about when they'd nab the next one.

I don't think they knew this part, but I could see it. I could see the little ways the divorce lawyers weren't actually incentivized to resolve conflict, but to escalate it. I could see the ways the criminal defense lawyers were incentivized to drag out cases longer and longer. I could see the ways the estate planning lawyers were incentivized to get their plans done more and more quickly, while at the same time leaving many holes in those plans for their clients. I could see the ways that it was the same for the business lawyers. Quick incorporations, and then on to the next, without any real guidance to the business owner that would help to grow their business, just waiting for the business owner to call with a problem that could have been prevented in the first place.

Obviously, they weren't actually helping their clients in the best way possible. But, it wasn't their fault, they just really didn't see another way. It was what we had been taught.

The traditional, transactional, and litigation-focused models aren't good for your clients, and they aren't good for you either.

This really hit home one night when I was out to dinner with my husband, and our three-year-old daughter was at home with our sixteen-year-old babysitter. In the middle of our perfectly lovely meal, I had the jarring thought:

What would happen if my husband and I never made it home?

I had written a will that named guardians for my daughter, but the family members I'd named lived across the country, more than 3,000 miles away. If something happened to us, and the authorities knocked on our door to find our daughter in the care of our babysitter, how would they find our will, anyway? Even once they did, they would have no choice but to take our child into the care of strangers until they could figure out how to reach my mom or sister—who would then need to fly across the country.

I was an estate lawyer, for crying out loud, but my own estate plan was seriously deficient for my own child. Even though I had done it all *right*, and certainly the way every lawyer I knew was doing it, my plan was unacceptable.

I suddenly understood that in order to create a new kind of estate plan for myself and others, I needed to rethink everything I had been taught.

To become the lawyer I wanted to be, I would need to reinvent the way legal services were provided to parents and business owners like me. A new law business model. I had to look beyond what I had learned in law school and in other lawyers' firms. So I reached out to business owners and entrepreneurs in other industries—truly successful business people who were doing work they were proud to do. It wasn't until I studied the methodologies of these service professionals—dentists, chiropractors, ophthalmologists, auto mechanics, carpet cleaners, and even a magician (whom I will tell you about later)—that I began to put the pieces together.

These professionals, with jobs and lives they loved, all had one thing in common: they relied on systems to automate some of their work, freeing up time for them to focus on building relationships with their clients.

The *systems* facilitated the *relationships* that were the key to delivering the best possible service.

Of course, there were plenty of estate planning lawyers out there who had created systematized law practices. The most "successful," i.e., high-earning, among them had hyper-structured their workflows to the point of being able to see a thousand clients a year.

But was that really success? Would the plans they were creating even work for their clients' families? From my experience in trying to untangle my father-in-law's botched planning, as well as my discovery that my *own* estate plan did not properly plan for the well-being of my daughter, I already knew the answer to that: they would not. Because as lawyers, it seems we had been trained to put *money* before impact.

I would come to learn that this fatal flaw, this disconnection from our own humanity and that of our clients, was also common among lawyers who served business owners. Again and again, I would see it cause business lawyers to serve their clients in a way that would ultimately fail those clients, and sometimes even destroy their hopes and dreams as a result. So, while I initially focused on reforming my estate planning practice, I would soon teach myself to serve business owners in a new way, too.

THE "CRAZY" NEW LAW BUSINESS MODEL

When I first started talking to other lawyers about my dream of inventing a new model for practicing law—a model that would allow me to have a life and law practice that I loved, a reasonable schedule, and clients who happily paid for my services because I was making a real difference in their lives—they said I was crazy.

They said I would starve.

They said if I focused my practice on serving young families and charging a premium for my services, I would go out of business.

They said young families and new business owners (the two groups of clients I was clear I wanted to serve once I got very focused with my marketing) wouldn't pay premium fees. They were too far from death, or too insecure about their businesses. I should just stick with the program and serve elders or established businesses.

But I wasn't fazed. Having talked to all those business owners in other industries, I had realized that my law degree was an incredibly valuable asset—one that the typical business owner did not have, and that I could use to turn my vision into a reality.

I knew those skeptical lawyers were wrong. They didn't see what I did: a gaping hole in the legal market that left families, just like mine, with legal plans that would fail their families when they needed them. A hole that left business owners woefully unsupported with their legal, insurance, financial, and tax foundations.

I knew there was a win-win model available for lawyers and their clients, if I could just figure out what it was, and implement it in my own community.

I would have to start by getting rid of what was broken about the way we were taught to serve clients and build law practices. From there, I could create something new.

Within three years, I had done it. I had created a brand-new way of educating my community and serving clients in my own office (what is now the *New Law Business Model)* and built a million-dollar law practice around its principles. I didn't starve like those other lawyers said I would. Quite the opposite, I had succeeded in creating a lucrative and impactful new niche focus of serving families with young children.

In my fourth year of practice, thanks to the *New Law Business Model* systems I'd created, I only had to go into my office three to four days a week, and I was still able to bring in more than a million dollars of revenue a year. Confident that I was on to something, I began devoting more of my time to educating families and business owners about why they needed the right kind of legal plan, done the *New Law Business Model* way.

I was able to earn so much revenue and work in the office so little because I had trained other lawyers in my office to begin educating the community and engaging the clients, which told me that the model I'd created would work for other lawyers too, not just for me.

I wrote a book called *Wear Clean Underwear: A Fast, Fun,*

Friendly—and Essential—Guide to Legal Planning for Busy Parents and appeared on the *Today Show, Good Morning America* and many other programs about the importance of effective estate planning and why most plans fail.

Reading all this now, it may sound as if it was easy, but it wasn't. I was learning some very expensive lessons the hard way—trial and error.

Although I'd built a million-dollar-a-year law practice, knew how to market it to get clients to hire me, and even knew how to get the work done, it wasn't enough. To maintain a million-dollar law practice requires so much more than that. It requires an understanding of how to handle money and people that was far beyond me at the time.

As my practice grew, so did my overhead. And since I didn't know how to manage the numbers, I was always worried about whether I would have enough to pay the bills.

I also didn't know how to manage the people part of my law practice. So, as my team grew, so did the conflicts. I often found myself getting frustrated and short-tempered.

I did feel successful in many ways. But in many *more* ways, I felt trapped. That's why, instead of continuing to grow my practice, I sabotaged it. I sold it to the wrong buyer, who immediately fired the marketing director and stopped running our ads (because he thought they were too expensive) and then wondered why he wasn't getting any new clients.

As a result, I got to see what makes the difference between a million-dollar business owner and one who isn't. He didn't have the business sense to keep writing the checks that were responsible for bringing in all the clients. So, once he'd stripped out all the profits, he handed me back the firm with a $250,000 debt to take on, if I wanted to do right by my clients and team, which I did. I ran the practice for six months without taking on any new clients to ensure my old clients would be properly transitioned to other lawyers I had trained, and to ensure my team wasn't left hanging without notice.

After I was hit with another $100,000 debt (as a result of my poor tax planning, which is part of what led me to see how much business owners need great counsel), and even though I had built a *second* million-dollar-grossing business, I decided to throw in the towel on all of it. I moved to a farm and filed bankruptcy. You've probably fantasized about doing that yourself along the way. Well, I actually did it.

It was a terrible time for me, but I'm happy to say that I wouldn't change it if I could. In the process, I got to realize that business owners need more than just lawyers who incorporate their businesses and send them on their way; they need comprehensive guidance on insurance, financial systems, and taxes—and we lawyers are the best ones to provide it, once we are well-trained ourselves. But not all of us should have to learn the hard way.

As a result of the trial and error that created my huge losses, and my willingness to stick with the *New Law* model until I understood it through and through, thousands of lawyers across the world are now serving families and business owners in a way that is impactful, meaningful, and a win-win for them and their clients.

Each year, I hear from more and more lawyers who are discovering the *New Law Business Model* and applying it in their own communities, with life-changing results for themselves and their clients. And, you can do this too, without the huge losses, of course. ☺

CHANGE YOUR LAW, CHANGE YOUR LIFE

Remember Richard? The litigator I told you about earlier who realized, mid-fist-pump, that he had become someone he never wanted to be—someone who was gleefully ruining his opposing counsel's Christmas?

Today, Richard has a thriving practice helping families stay out of court with estate planning that actually works. Instead of using his law degree to keep people embroiled in escalating conflict or just creating form documents for clients (which he knows won't work when the family needs them), Richard gets to educate his community with the heart of a teacher, gets paid well to be a counselor, and is using his law practice to make people's lives better.

Richard stopped ruining holidays a long time ago, and now he looks forward to spending every one of them with his family.

If you think Richard's wallet has suffered, think again: Richard is *taking home* $250,000 a year, working three-and-a-half days a week in his office.

I can't tell you how much I love hearing about the life-changing results the *New Law Business Model* has had for burned-out, disillusioned lawyers like Richard. Their stories debunk the myth of the stereotypical, self-absorbed, money-grubbing lawyer. They affirm what *we* know, even if the rest of the world doesn't: most of us lawyers have huge hearts, or we wouldn't be doing what we do.

Law is a helping profession. I wasn't always sure about this myself, honestly. And I had to re-find my own heart to know it to be true.

You went to school to make the world a better place. You want to do a great job. You want to help people. You are a good human stuck in a broken system.

MAKING LAW RELATIONAL

Before you continue to invest more time reading this book, you might wonder where the *New Law Business Model* really works the best—or whether it will work with your practice area or in your community.

The *New Law Business Model* works in all communities where people care what happens to their families, friends, and businesses if they become incapacitated or when they die. And it works best for lawyers who truly want to make a difference in their clients' lives, make a great living, and have complete control over their schedule while they do it.

The *New Law Business Model* takes what was formerly *transactional* and makes it *relational*. The model uses predictable, repeatable systems that deliver consistent results to create a highly personalized, yet efficient and even surprisingly affordable result for the people you serve. The model gives you the time, energy and attention to be a true counselor and advisor to your clients.

The model is systemized, yet each client has the experience of feeling as if the system was created just for them. It is ideal for lawyers who want to serve families and/or small business owners, though many elements of the model can be applied to law practices that serve clients in other practice areas, such as divorce, bankruptcy, real estate, and immigration.

If you work in one of the areas I've just mentioned, I believe you will find elements of the *New Law Business Model* to be an asset to your work. I also hope, by the way, that it might inspire you to consider bringing estate and/or business planning into your practice—even if you hated your trusts and estates class in law school.

WHY SERVE FAMILIES AND SMALL BUSINESS OWNERS?

According to data from the Census Bureau's Annual Survey of Entrepreneurs, there were 5.6 million employer businesses in the United States in 2016. Businesses with fewer than 500 workers accounted for 99.7 percent of those businesses. Every single one of those businesses and their owners needs wise counsel, not just on incorporation or contract review or employment agreements. They also need a lawyer who can keep them out of court in the event of a conflict. They also need a lawyer who can help them make good, proactive decisions about all of their legal, insurance, financial, and tax matters. With the right training, that could be you.

On the estate planning side, I've got a secret to share with you. It's one you already know, but might not have considered, fully:

Every single person you know is going to die. And, before that, they may become incapacitated for some period of time.

And while not all of the people you know need a fancy estate plan with all the bells and whistles, eventually *every single adult human you know needs to have something in place to keep their loved ones out of court and out of conflict, in the event of their incapacity or when they die*. Period.

You've got a huge opportunity to educate your community about the practical realities of incapacity and death, and how facing it squarely and wisely during life actually creates more and better life.

You have an opportunity to get families talking about things that are often not talked about until it's too late, and to help business owners (if you choose to serve them) to stay out of conflict in their businesses, and instead grow their families and their dreams. To me, this is the greatest gift you can give your community as a lawyer.

Now, I know this is not what we were taught in law school about life and death and business, but that's also why it's such a huge opportunity for you. When you get in touch with the reality of what estate planning is really about and how to talk about that with your community in a new way, you get to totally differentiate yourself from other lawyers, and you can never be replaced by technology.

What we're talking about here is personal, relational, and the most human work you can do. This has nothing to do with complex tax transactions or helping the rich get even richer. This has everything to do with life, death, legacy, and inheritance. As I said, it affects *every single human being you know.*

On the financial side, within the next fifteen years, one-fifth of the population will be over the age of sixty-five, and as this generation passes on, there will be a $41 trillion transfer of wealth. During the next thirty years, ninety-three million people will transfer their assets to the next generation.

Beyond the baby boomer generation, consider that every single adult who has a family or owns something needs a plan for their estate. No one escapes death, and everyone wants to be sure their assets are transitioned properly. The opportunity is enormous and growing. This is not a morbid conversation, but it is an emotional one.

I have found that people who plan for death during life, and talk to their loved ones about their planning, are happier and more secure. They don't enter old age worrying about what will happen to their belongings and financial assets or how their families will manage without them. In the ideal situation—and with your help—these conversations will happen early and often, providing significant peace of mind and creating harmonious families whose members will support one another for generations, instead of breaking up due to poor communication around critical matters.

And people are becoming ready and willing to face these issues younger and younger in life.

As I shared earlier, when I first started my practice, I decided to focus on serving families with young children. All the other lawyers who had been doing estate planning for years said I was nuts to do it. But I knew this new practice area was needed and wanted because I was a young mother myself, and I knew there was nothing more important to me than doing the right thing by my children.

I wasn't at all surprised to discover that many, many young parents felt just as I did.

If you want to hear more specifics about how we are serving these families the *New Law* way, I recommend you check out the many resources compiled at newlawbusinessmodel. com/resources.

For now, what I want you to know is that serving business owners and families (young or old) with estate planning the *New Law Business Model* way is needed and wanted. When you follow our guidelines for educating your community and serving your clients, you will not (cannot) be replaced by technology. Your law practice will be immune to any economic downturns coming our way.

One of the lawyers I trained early on, Dee, started her

practice right before the 2008 recession, and grew steadily through it with our systems, even while taking two maternity leaves over a three-year period. Today, she has a million-dollar-a-year law practice. And, so does David. He joined us right before the recession began, in 2007, and today he's *the* go-to lawyer for parents in Acton, Massachusetts.

If you've been practicing one type of law for years and think it's too late to make a switch or to add on new services, think ahead a couple of years.

Technological unemployment, the loss of jobs caused by technological innovation, is coming for lawyers. If you do not differentiate yourself from your competition, you will face the reality of having to decrease your fees more and more to compete with automation. You already know this, but perhaps you've been burying your head in the sand to avoid it.

So, again, let's look out into the future of your life and law practice. Do you want to be exactly where you are now—working too much, not making the hugely positive impact you know is possible, unfulfilled by your life as a lawyer?

Or could you consider making a change that will deliver a whole new experience to your community in a short time?

You have a choice.

If you're a new grad or getting ready to graduate from law school, there is no transition required. You can start building your law practice with the *New Law Business Model* right now.

If you're worried about starting a law practice, remember: you have a law degree. And when you know how to use it, it's your most valuable asset. Most new business owners aren't so lucky. They start their businesses from scratch, having to figure out a service to offer, how to price and package their service, how to create demand for it, how to find their clients, and how to actually deliver their service.

You don't have to figure any of that out. My team and I at the *New Law Business Model* have done it all for you. And you have a built-in market, just waiting for you to educate them about achieving their dreams before death, and how to pass along a lasting legacy to their loved ones.

There really is an incredible, life-changing power and potential in your law degree, *if you know how to use it*.

Wherever you are in your legal career, you can become one of a small percentage of lawyers who are true, trusted advisors to clients who actively seek them out. You can set your own hours, make a fantastic income, do amazing work—and you can love your life, too.

You don't have to waste another day wondering if you did the right thing going to law school (if you have been wondering that); you've made it here, and that's your first step to meaningful change. But there is one thing you'll need to have firmly in place to actually apply the program I offer you here. So, let's check in on that before we go any further.

YOUR COMMITMENT

Making a transition from whatever you are doing right now to educating your community and serving your clients in a new way will require your commitment.

When I created the *New Law Business Model*, I was supporting a family—and I was *terrified*. How could I go from a steady six-figure salary with benefits at one of the most prestigious law firms in the country, to the unknown of my own law practice? I didn't come from a wealthy family and I had no backup or support system in place. I didn't have to know how it would work out or where the money would come from to make the investments I did to start and grow my law practice.

I took the leap of faith anyway, and learned a critical lesson as I did: when you commit to what you really want, even if you do not have the clarity on *how* it will happen or *where* the resources will come from—when you get clear on *what* you want—all of the resources show up.

When you're committed, you look for solutions. If you're not, you look for excuses.

This is important, because you can easily shortchange yourself by getting hung up on the *how* and the *money* (or what you may perceive as the lack of it*)*. But the *how* doesn't matter, at first. **What matters is your 100 percent commitment to creating success on your own terms, no matter what. Period. End of story.**

Commitment before clarity may be the one lesson I've learned that has served me more than anything else in my life.

Every single time I have committed to making a change in my life, the clarity I needed for my next steps appeared. Then the resources I needed appeared, often from the most unexpected places.

So, as you are reading the rest of this book, I will invite you to keep coming back to your commitment.

Are you committed to having a life and law practice you love? If so, why? Anchor that *why* into your full being, because it's what's going to pull you through all the hard parts that come along as you transform your life and law practice. Without a strong *why*, you'll just revert back to the way you've always done things and make excuses about why you can't change.

Your *why* is the foundation of your commitment. You'll want to refer back to this when the going gets tough and you need a reminder of why it's worth it to keep moving forward, keep referring to this book, and keep making the investments needed to change your life.

Even if you aren't yet sure why you must build a life and law practice you love, keep reading. The answers will come.

So, let's talk about that sometimes elusive *why,* and then we'll get to the intimidating word that keeps so many of us from acting on our dreams: *how.*

CHAPTER TWO

ANCHORING IN YOUR WHY AND HOW

"If you're serious about becoming a wealthy, powerful, sophisticated, healthy, influential, cultured and unique individual, keep a journal—don't trust your memory. When you listen to something valuable, write it down. When you come across something important, write it down."

—JIM ROHN, ENTREPRENEUR, 1930-2009

The entrepreneurial mindset is one that requires you to get extremely clear on what you want, and then make your decisions *from that place of clarity* instead of from where you are now. If you keep making your decisions from where you are now, you're going to keep getting what you've always gotten. Instead, **you must shift into a mindset of making your decisions from where you want to be.** And that requires you to be able to clearly see that future, put yourself into it, and then work backwards to the choices you will make today to create it.

There's no better tool for finding the clarity you want and need than a journal. Go to newlawbusinessmodel.com/resources to find a free gift we have for you to support your journaling process.

So, before you read any further, if you have not already, grab a pen and a notebook. I want you to write down: thoughts that arise about *why* you want to transition away from the way you are currently using your law degree; and ideas that occur to you about *how* you can transition using the *New Law Business Model*.

Thoughts and ideas can be fleeting, and you may think you'll remember them when you need them, but you probably won't. Something you read here may spark an important thought or a fantastic idea, and you want to capture it while it's fresh, before it flits away.

If I had not journaled constantly while I was creating my business, I don't believe much of what I have created would ever have happened.

Your journal or notebook doesn't need to be fancy. A legal pad or steno notebook will do. I've got stacks of steno notebooks filled with ideas from my early days of practice.

Writing down your thoughts—no matter how vague or flimsy they may seem right now—makes it all *real*. The things you write down now will be easier to commit to later, and your chances of actually making them happen will improve exponentially.

We're going to start to anchor in your *why* by reflecting on something that's even more important than your law practice: why you went to law school in the first place.

WHY YOU WENT TO LAW SCHOOL

Take a few moments to really think about what made you choose to become a lawyer.

- Did you want to make a difference in the world?
- Did you have a cause in mind, such as having a long-lasting, positive effect on people's lives?
- Did you want your life to have an impact—to *matter*?
- Maybe you did, or maybe you studied law because you didn't know *what* to do and law sounded like a good option.
- Plus, you figured it was a profession that would allow you to make a lot of money.
- Maybe you just didn't know what else to do and figured law school would be a good idea.

None of these answers are wrong. No matter why you went to law school, your reason is valid and perfectly acceptable.

Title the first page in your notebook like this:

Why I Went to Law School

Now write down *all* your reasons. You may have one, or you may have many. Get them all out there—every single one.

Read them back to yourself, one at a time. Think about each one. Are those reasons still important to you? Do you still have the same wants, needs, values, and aspirations that you had when you decided to become a lawyer?

If you became a lawyer to have a positive impact on society, or on a particular section of society, how is that playing out for you? Have you had to sacrifice making a decent income in order to practice the kind of law that makes that possible? Or, have you had to sacrifice your values, instead, and give up on your higher aspirations so you can make money?

You've likely settled somehow. If you are still tied to a BigLaw firm, you are probably getting a regular paycheck, but that steady money is coming at the expense of your personal life, and possibly even your ability to sleep well at night.

If you are practicing alone or in a small firm, your cash

flow is probably unpredictable and stressful, regardless of how much money you're earning. Some months, the money flows, but there are other months when there isn't enough and you lie awake at night, wondering if the next month will be different. You could take on more clients to ease the financial stress, but that adds another kind of stress. Besides, can you—one person—realistically serve a significant number of clients in a way that's meaningful and helpful?

The answer to that is a resounding yes, and I'll tell you why soon. But first, let's go deeper into what's not working for you—and for your clients—right now.

WHAT'S NOT WORKING

You may want to write something to this effect at the top of the next page in your journal:

What's Not Working for My Life, My
Law Practice, and My Clients

First, think about what isn't working for you professionally.

- Do you want to feel more appreciated by your clients?
- Are you constantly chasing invoices?
- Do you invest in lead services that send you clients who don't hire you?

- Do the clients who *do* hire you use your services on a "one-off" basis instead of staying with you long term?
- Do you wish you had a way to vet your clients and encourage them to stay with you long term so you could serve them better?
- Do you wish you had a way to educate your community about the law?
- Are you excited about how you could be leveraging technology in your practice, but you don't even know where to start?
- Or does all this new technology terrify you because it could put you out of business?

Then, answer this question:

What might I be doing now that truly is not best for my clients?

- Do you escalate conflict for your clients so you can bill more hours and earn more money for yourself? (Be honest.)
- Do you take on clients for whom you may *not be* the best fit, simply because you need to pay the bills?
- Do you feel as if you need to churn through clients, all the while suspecting that you may not be providing the best service for them?
- Have you put wills, trusts, and business plans in place knowing that if a situation arose—such as the death or incapacitation of your client or some kind of legal action

against your client's business—your legal documents would not provide the service and protection your clients will need?

- Do you constantly wonder where your next clients will come from and make your choices from a place of scarcity?

Spend some more time now looking at what isn't working for you, your clients, and your business.

Don't skip over this part; it's *critically* important that you get 100 percent crystal clear on this.

No one is going to see this notebook except for you, so be brutally honest with yourself. Write down all the things that have been bothering you about your practice of law, even if you've been afraid to put them into words up until now.

It will feel good to get these thoughts out and on paper, like a deep breath and an exhale—a release. You are not the only lawyer who has had realizations like these.

I want you to hang onto these pages. You can add to them later as new thoughts arise.

For now, congratulate yourself: the first step to facing and moving beyond your shortcomings is to acknowledge them.

This brings us to a very important next step in your process.

SEE HOW "LAWYER SHAME" MAY BE BLOCKING YOUR SUCCESS

Okay, let's go to the next page in your notebook. We'll call this page *Guilt and Shame*. It's time to face a tough, ugly truth that lawyers don't like to talk about. We are going to surface this truth, root it out, and face it head-on so that you can see where it's sabotaging your success, and release it once and for all.

So, here it is:

Many people think lawyers are crooks and liars.

Ugh, there it is. I said it. Take a deep breath now and let's get through this bit.

We need to face the reality that lawyers have a bad reputation and some of us well deserve it, but most of us do not. Regardless, we all have to deal with it.

And also recognize where our own feelings of guilt and shame could be creating behaviors that reinforce this bad reputation, inadvertently.

It's time to break the cycle and reclaim your rightful role as a helper, an advisor, a teacher, and a counselor. And to do that, we need to look at where you may have been taught bad habits and practices that reinforce the bad rap we lawyers get.

It does *not* have to be this way. You can break those bad habits, and set yourself free. When you are practicing law with the *New Law Business Model* in place, you will be proud of the work you are doing and have 100 percent confidence that you are truly serving people in your community.

So, let's look at where the guilt or shame around the way you've been taught could be showing up in your law practice right now.

Look back at what you wrote in your notebook under *What's Not Working for My Life, My Law Practice, and My Clients* and see where you may be engaging in behaviors that are actually not that awesome for you or your clients.

Anywhere that you are not 100 percent confident that the service you are providing to your clients is top-notch, best in class, and truly impactful, you are likely going to hold back from having the success you really want. At least that's the case if you truly have a good heart. And if you don't truly have a good heart, this book isn't for you.

My guess is that you do have shame about the way you are

practicing (consciously or unconsciously), and that shame may be showing up as the persistent thought: I don't want people to feel as if I am trying to sell them on my services.

This train of thought is insidious and if not handled by you, it will sabotage all of your efforts to build a meaningful life and law practice. We will handle this thought and I will provide you with solutions for it later in the book. For now, know that when you are practicing the *New Law Business Model*, you are never selling anything to anyone. Your job is to empower, educate, and inform people to make wise decisions for their families and businesses, and then have the systems in place to serve them, if hiring you is truly what they want and need.

Just notice if the thought, *I don't want people to feel as if I am trying to sell them on my services,* runs through your mind when you network, or speak, or meet new potential clients in your office.

If it does, consider whether you might be reluctant to educate others about your services because you don't actually believe, deep down, that your services are valuable.

This insecurity is all too common, and based in a secret shame (possibly justified) that prevents us lawyers from engaging fully with our clients, serving them at the highest level, and charging fees that allow us to provide the best service possible. It's a vicious cycle we have to break.

Here are some of the most common ways shame could be showing up in your law practice:

- You don't send invoices because you feel guilty about billing your time in six-minute increments, or because it's just more trouble than it's worth.
- You've got quite a lot of unpaid invoices out there, but you don't pursue payment aggressively and you aren't even sure why.
- You are afraid to get outside of the box and innovate your law practice away from what all the other lawyers are doing.
- You try to do everything yourself, falling more and more behind and feeling guilty as the work piles up with no light at the end of the tunnel.
- You want to be seen as being available, so you answer every phone call and email yourself and respond to text messages at all hours of the day and night—even though it's eating into your personal time.
- And again, the biggie: you are afraid of coming off as self-promotional, so you hold back from talking about what you do and how you can help people in your community.

Do any of these behaviors sound familiar to you?

If so, you're sacrificing your personal time to sustain a law practice that you're not actually proud of and that doesn't provide you with predictable cash flow—while telling yourself you're doing *what has to be done* to run your business.

I believe we have just discovered a whole new definition of insanity.

But it's likely that you will keep doing what you've always done, even though you know it's not what's best for you and your clients and may even cause you shame, because, as Jonathan Fields writes in *Uncertainty: Turning Fear and Doubt into Fuel for Brilliance*: "Fear of judgment stifles our ability to embrace uncertainty and as part of that process delivers a serious blow to our willingness to create anything that hasn't already been done and validated."

Now that you've considered where your fear of judgment or unwillingness to embrace uncertainty may be holding you back, I'm going to provide you with as much evidence as I can that the *New Law Business Model* will work for you. Still, all new things come with uncertainty. It will be up to you to embrace yours, in service to being the kind of lawyer you will feel proud to be.

TURN THE PAGE

Turn the page in your notebook to a fresh sheet of paper. Take another breath while you're at it. You've made it through the toughest part of this chapter and the rest is going to be a lot more fun.

Think about what your ideal life would look like as a lawyer. If you could paint a picture of truly living your best life and making a difference in your clients' lives, what would that look like?

Title the new page like this:

My Ideal Lawyer Life

Imagine it. You wake up every day excited to educate your community and serve your clients.

You have systems in place that enable you to serve your clients honestly and efficiently.

You have no shame, no guilt, and no worry whatsoever that everything you're doing will provide your clients with the legal services they want and need.

When you network in your community, meet with referral partners, or give a talk, you feel proud and confident. You consistently hear from the people you are meeting, "Hey, you don't seem like a lawyer. I'd love to work with you. How can we get started?"

Oh, and you're making more money than you will ever need—a *lot* more.

Imagine your dream law practice. Then, at the top of this fresh clean page in your notebook, write down the answers to these questions:

- What does your dream practice look like? Who are you serving? How are you helping them? What kinds of problems do you solve for them?
- How do you spend your work time? Are you out in the community, networking and speaking? Are you in your office meeting with clients? Or are you behind the computer, doing research and writing documents?
- Are you working solo, or do you have a team? Is your team big or small? How many people are there and what do they do? Do you have other attorneys working for you?

Now, imagine what your dream office looks like.

Are you in a high-rise, a strip mall, or do you have a standalone, homey office that fits in with the neighborhood?

Picture it all in your mind: the technology, the furniture, the lighting, the space. Imagine the front door of your office—what your clients see when they approach your building and your office. How big is your desk? Are there plants in the office? Is it pet friendly or no pets allowed? What's hanging on the walls? Your degrees? Artwork? Photos of your family?

Today, you may not even need to have a full-time office at all. You could work totally or partially virtually. Would that be most ideal for you? If so, what does your work-space look like? How do your ideal clients engage with you? What do they experience each step of the way in the virtual environment? You can be just as intentional here as you would be when designing your dream brick-and-mortar office.

Or maybe you split your time between a customer-facing office you share with your team and your home office?

If you're looking for design inspiration, you can take a video tour of the dream office I built when I first went into solo practice. It's at Newlawbusinessmodel.com/resources.

Now, what kind of schedule do you keep? How many days do you work each week, and how many hours do you work on those days?

Okay, let's get more personal.

- In your dream life and law practice, how much vacation time do you take each year?
- Do you take two weeks off every six months for an

extended vacation, sabbatical, or to hang out with your family?

- Do you take time away from your firm to bike, backpack, climb, trek, do yoga, or sail somewhere new and exotic?
- Or do you take a couple of weeks off and donate your time to a cause that's important to you?

Time for some of the nitty gritty details that are going to be a guiding north star for you as you build out your ideal law practice model:

- How much money do you want to take home each month (not bring in as gross revenue, but *take home*)?
- Why do you want to take home that much money?
- How will you use it?
- What will change in your life when you are bringing that much money home consistently?

And here's a very big question I want you to take some time to answer honestly, because it's this answer that's going to get you through the tough spots that come along in the future:

Why is all of this important to you?

Write it down. It's necessary to clarify *why* all of this matters to you—to be 100 percent crystal-freaking-clear on all of it. Clarity around why you want to make a change is critical because it is this clarity that will provide the courage you need to do what needs to be done when you are up against your fears, which are sure to rise up along the way.

As you come up against your fears or points where you need to do something that is outside your comfort zone, having clarity about what you are creating and most importantly, why you are creating it, will pull you through. If you are *not* clear on the *why*, your fear or discomfort will stop you in your tracks.

As you build your own law practice with the *New Law Business Model*, you will need to navigate some pretty colossal fears. And here's a little hint: if you aren't navigating fear on a regular basis, chances are you aren't on the right path.

Sometimes, it can be difficult to see fear, and we'll talk more about how to spot it and what to do with it a bit later in the book.

For now, though, let's discuss one very obvious fear you'll face when building your *New Law* practice: the fear that the significant investments you are making in this process might not pay off.

That's terrifying, right?! It was for me.

And, if my *why* had not been bigger than my fear, I never

would have done it. I would have stayed small, scared, and in my comfort zone. Heck, I'd probably still be at the BigLaw firm, doing work I didn't really believe in for a paycheck that kept me in false comfort.

Writing down your dreams and then returning to those writings when you get scared and need a reminder of *what* you want and *why* you want it is *key* to surmounting your fears around creating the law practice you want and deserve.

Ultimately...

"The fears we don't face become our limits."

—ROBIN SHARMA

If you want to read the full story of how my unfaced fears limited me to the point that I was driven into bankruptcy, and what I learned through the process, visit newlawbusinessmodel.com and search for "Why did Alexis file bankruptcy?"

MONEY MAP YOUR WAY TO A LIFE AND LAW PRACTICE YOU LOVE

By now, your notebook may be filled with ideas about the life and law practice you want to have. And you are ready to get even more clear and specific with a plan for getting there. I've created a resource based on my own experience to help.

The *Money Map for Lawyers* program, which I'm about to tell you about and give you for free, is something I wish I'd had when I was first starting out on my own.

After I sabotaged my first two million-dollar businesses and filed for bankruptcy, I moved to a farm to reconnect with who I was. I spent a year doing nothing I wouldn't do for free and figuring out what really mattered to me, and where my dream had gone wrong.

One of my biggest epiphanies: I had been suffering from what I now know as "money dysmorphia." Money dysmorphia is the distorted view of our financial reality that tells us we will never, ever have enough. It's a scarcity mentality that's rooted in our ancestral patterns around survival and perpetuated by the media as well as the financial services industry.

I believe that money dysmorphia is a common disease, and it's driving the human race towards extinction by causing us to make poor decisions about how we spend our time, energy, attention, and money (TEAM) resources. Our fear of not having enough causes us to squander our invaluable *nonrenewable resources*—time, energy, and attention—in constant pursuit of the one resource that is truly renewable, money.

Only when we recognize our money dysmorphia can we begin to make the shift from a paradigm of not-enoughness to one of abundance and generosity. How do we do this? The first step is to get comfortable with money math and business numbers.

This was no baby step for me. It was a huge leap. I went to law school (partially) because I was bad at math, and numbers and spreadsheets scared me.

To guide myself through that fear, I created a straightforward tool that helped me get *super* clear about what I needed to be doing and focusing on each month, week, day, and even hour of my life.

That tool became the *Money Map to Freedom* program, which is a $5,000 training available through my other company, Eyes Wide Open. Because I see money mapping as a critical first step in gaining clarity around whether the *New Law Business Model* is for you, I'm giving you a free mini-version of that program, made just for lawyers.

It makes me feel a whole lot better about my bankruptcy to know that the *Money Map* to *Freedom* and the *Money Map for Lawyers* came out of it.

Whether or not you decide to go all the way with the *New Law Business Model*, the *Money Map for Lawyers* will help you start to make conscious choices about how you're using your TEAM (time, energy, attention and money) resources. It will show you exactly how many clients you need each month, and at what average fee, in order to build the practice model that you really, really, really want, while rapidly achieving your personal financial and time goals.

I think you'll especially love the Cash Flow Forecasting Tool, which will help you create a detailed financial projection of your future cash flow, so you can pick a law practice model that works best for your current law practice, your family reality, how much money you want to make, and the time you actually have to create it all.

And if you are working with a team, the *Money Map for Lawyers* program will also help you clearly communicate your immediate and big picture targets and goals for the practice, so everyone can work together to support those goals.

No more sleepless nights worrying about what you should be doing. It's time to convert that wasted energy into concrete action steps.

If you want all that, get started with the *Money Map for Lawyers* right now. Go to moneymapforlawyers.com and enter your name and email for immediate, free access.

Then, head on over to Module 1, watch the training video, download your workbook, and block an hour on your calendar to do the assignments. It's going to be the best hour you spend on your law practice this week. And then you'll be ready to pick your path to the most ideal law practice model for you.

Ready to find your practice model? Let's go!

CHAPTER THREE

PICK YOUR IDEAL PRACTICE MODEL

YOUR LIFE, YOUR LAW PRACTICE

A clear vision of the life and law practice you want will support you to have the greatest success with the *New Law Business Model,* or in any and all areas of your life, really. Clarity is everything. Your clarity of vision will provide you with a target to set your sights on, and open a clear path between your current situation and your ideal life.

That's why I've identified three practice models that fit the realities of what most lawyers want to create for their lives. Choosing the right model will get you from where you are right now to where you want to be quickly and efficiently, with a clear goal in mind, and without spinning your wheels.

After all, it's easy to say, "I want to have a million-dollar-a-year law practice," because that's what you think success means. But if that desire is not actually aligned with the personal life you really want, the clients you want to serve, the team you want to build, and the hours you want to work, you will constantly chase it in vain—hurting your confidence, income, and reputation along the way.

On the flip side, if you *do* somehow get to a million-dollar-a-year practice that doesn't align with your other life goals, you'll find yourself with a law practice that sucks all of your life force energy, leaves you with no free time, and creates constant worry about whether you can keep all the balls in the air to maintain the monster you've created.

Had I clearly defined my law practice model when I first went into business for myself, I would have either built my practice to sell, and sold it the right way, to the right person, or I would have built it as a part-time practice that would be thriving today, earning me a nice ongoing income and serving families and small business owners in my former community.

Instead...well, you know what happened.

The good news is that I was able to rebuild successfully, and today my law practice is exactly the right size for me. I work (virtually) with just one to three clients a month who pay me between $2,500 and $10,000 per month to be their trusted advisor at a very high level. I'm able to do that from my home in Colorado, while I operate as CEO of the companies that I created, and still stay present for my teenage children and extended community. I made this possible by identifying and implementing the *Solo Practitioner* model of practice, one of the three you're about to see up close.

DO YOU WANT TO BE A *TRUE SOLO*, A *PART-TIME LAW BALLER*, OR A *7-FIGURE LAW PRACTICE EMPIRE BUILDER*?

Okay, here we go—the three main practice models used by *New Law Business Model* lawyers.

THE *SOLO PRACTITIONER* (ALSO CALLED WORK FROM HOME PRO OR TRUE SOLO MODEL)

The *Solo Practitioner* works alone or with a part-time or virtual assistant out of her home or office, serving between one and four clients a month. For most lawyers who attempt to work solo without clear guidance and support, their practice quickly takes over their lives. But it doesn't have to be that way, if you set it up right.

Working Solo the Old Way

The *Solo Practitioner* working the *old* way is trying to see three to four or maybe even more clients a month without an assistant, outsourcing, or the right systems in place. She is working way too much, and has no energy left over to create anything meaningful with the free time she does have. Because she doesn't have a clear idea of what she's supposed to be doing every day, she ends up putting in many more hours than she expected—and far more than are necessary—to get new clients every month and serve them on her own. She constantly feels as if she's scrambling to keep up—answering every phone call and every email—yet she never has enough income to show for it. Working solo becomes extremely stressful, and there's no light at the end of the tunnel.

The *Solo Practitioner*: The *New Law Business Model* Way

With systems in place, the *Solo Practitioner* working the *New Law* way can comfortably attract and serve four clients a month. Because her community outreach *systems* empower her to generate appointments with truly motivated prospects, she is not taking dead-end meetings and has the time and energy to do an excellent job for everyone she serves. She keeps a nine-to-five schedule, and actually enjoys her life.

Like the sound of working as a *Solo Practitioner*? Let's take a closer look.

First things first: if your goal is to take home $10,000 per month, you'll need to generate at least $240,000 per year in total gross revenue. I know: ouch. But this won't work unless you see clearly, remember? Most lawyers who want to generate $10,000 per month seem to have a weird belief that they only need to generate $10,000 per month, and, of course that's hugely flawed thinking.

I get it, of course. I thought things like that myself when I didn't really understand business.

But with systems in place to educate your community (through expos, networking that works, and speaking engagements that pay off, plus follow-up systems and technology), you can consistently attract, engage, and serve four new clients a month at an average fee of $3,000 to $5,000 each with estate planning that truly serves; or, if you are serving business owners as a strategic business advisor, that average fee will be $750 to $3,000 per month. This will allow you to hit your financial goals—and do it working virtually or from home, if you choose.

Let's look even closer at the numbers, so you can see it even more clearly. Four clients, at an average fee of $4,000 will bring you $16,000 per month.

Set aside $3,000 for taxes, and start to consider how you could invest $3,000 per month to bring in those four clients each month, steadily and predictably, and to serve them really well, with as much support for you and as many systems as possible.

Please note that I said, "With as much support and as many systems as possible."

The *New Law Business Model* is not about you spending as little as possible building your law practice, whichever practice model you choose. It's about you having as much *support* as possible, so you can leverage your law degree to provide a truly meaningful service that cannot be handled by robots or AI in the future, while earning what you need to live happily in the now.

With four clients a month, you can keep $10,000 a month. And, if you get a little more support, and increase those four clients to five or six, now you can afford even more support, and really start to free up your most valuable asset, your time.

Case Study: Rebecca

The *Solo Practitioner* practice is perfectly embodied by Rebecca. She started working with the *New Law Business Model* several years ago, knowing she didn't want anything more than a part-time practice because she's a full-time mom. Rebecca was already doing basic wills and trusts, and she wanted to do it well and have a business that complemented her life.

Having transitioned to her new model, Rebecca is able to focus on her practice when she needs to focus on her practice. When she's with her kids, she can focus solely on being with them.

Unlike many lawyers who try to work from home, Rebecca isn't feeling guilty when she's working, thinking she should be spending time with her family; and when she's with her family, her mind's not on work.

Rebecca brings home her target income, while working with the number of clients she can comfortably serve well, which for Rebecca is a maximum of four new clients a month.

Rebecca is able to do this successfully because she learned how to use expos and strategic networking, plus follow-up systems to consistently communicate with the people she meets and generate consistent business, instead of just wasting her time. To see Rebecca's highly effective expo booth, go to newlawbusinessmodel.com/resources.

Rebecca started by learning how to get hired by every prospect she spends time with (weeding out those who do not need her services before ever scheduling a two-hour Family Wealth Planning Session—our version of an initial consultation) for an average fee of $3,500 to $5,500 per client.

Finally, Rebecca is not going it alone or reinventing the

wheel. She licenses the *New Law Business Model* done-for-you marketing resources, weekly email newsletters, website copy, *Wear Clean Underwear* book, and done-for-you presentations to educate her community. Her day-to-day practice is streamlined using our all-in-one automated practice management technology solution.

If Rebecca had to create, try, and test all of that on her own, she'd have had to invest a lot more time in her practice; and while she might have been saving money in theory, it would actually cost her a lot more in the long run. Her kids are only young once, and the time she sacrifices trying to reinvent the wheel *could* cost her their childhood.

Case Study: Irene

Not all *Solo Practitioners* have children at home, though. Irene, for example, came from a very different situation. After raising her children and being a nurse for thirty years, Irene attended law school late in life. In a way, legal practice was her third career.

In her fifties and fresh out of law school, Irene was eager to start her own practice. At the same time, her husband was preparing for a job transfer from Orlando to Tennessee, so Irene wanted to build a virtual law practice that wouldn't be affected by the move.

Irene hadn't done any prior legal work when she came to the *New Law Business Model*, yet within one year, she had a thriving estate planning practice. Her *Solo Practitioner* model was mostly virtual. Irene very quickly began to see an average of four clients a month, all within the same week. She then spent another week working in her at-home practice and didn't work at all two weeks out of every month. She structured it that way because she was splitting time between her home in Orlando and her husband's new work location in Tennessee.

Irene was able to maintain this structure because just about everyone she talks to wants to meet with her to find out more about her services. She has learned how to educate prospective clients about what it really means to have a functional estate plan—i.e., one that will be updated throughout the client's lifetime, prevent their children from being taken into the care of strangers, and keep their loved ones out of court. Irene has an intake, follow-up, and initial meeting process that results in every client who sits down with her hiring her at an average fee of $4,500 each.

Four clients per month, $18,000 on average per month, working just two weeks out of the month.

But then, Irene's husband, Hector, who is also a lawyer, went and changed everything. He'd been nonpracticing for many years, and when he saw Irene's success, he decided to leave his corporate work and join her in practice! Irene and Hector have now moved back to Florida, have two offices, and are building a staffed practice together (see the *Staffed Practice* model, below). But first, do you want to hear directly from Irene about the *Solo Practitioner* model and how she did it? Join our private Facebook group, and you'll find my interview with Irene there. You can join our Facebook group at newlawbusinessmodel.com/awesomelawyers.

Is the Solo Practitioner Model for You?

The *Solo Practitioner* model is a great place to start your transition into the *New Law Business Model*, whether you intend to eventually build a seven-figure empire, or you just want to get a side hustle going as you transition out of an unfulfilling law practice model that isn't currently working for you.

Before you can build something big, it often helps to start small. And if you can make-do on $10,000 a month take-home or less, it could be a great place to start. But do know that you won't really be "solo" in the traditional sense, because it just doesn't make sense for you to go it fully alone. There are far too many things that you don't need to be doing yourself, that you can easily outsource or have a very part-time or virtual assistant help you with, so that you can focus on the highest leverage activities that truly serve you and your community.

Once you know how to educate your community in a new way (which we'll discuss in more detail soon!) so that people want to work with you, you can either choose to stay small, working mostly virtually with a part-time assistant; or you can use your early success as a launching pad and confidently hire one or more people to support you.

To check out what a *Solo Practitioner* model pro forma plus a blocked calendar might look like, download our cash flow forecast and time-blocking calendar for a *Solo Practitioner* at newlawbusinessmodel.com/resources.

THE *PART-TIME LAW BALLER* (*STAFFED PRACTICE*) MODEL

The *Staffed Practice* model is a great model for lawyers who enjoy spending the majority of their time engaging directly with their clients, and only want to go into the office three-and-a-half days a week. If I was in private practice as my primary income model, this is what I would choose. With a support staff of three, the quintessential *Staffed Practice* works about three-and-a-half days a week, sees about twelve to fifteen clients a month, and brings home between $150,000 and $250,000 a year. You can see why we named it *Baller*, right?

This model does require investment in an office, a team, and for you to be hosting presentations in your community. But it's also the single most efficient way to create a law practice that does great work for your clients and allows you to go into the office just a few days a week, while bringing home up to $250,000 per year.

That sounds pretty great, right? A lot better than working part time the old way.

Working Part Time the Old Way

In my experience, many lawyers trying to work part time are doing it so inefficiently that they end up working full time and just getting paid for part time.

We see that a lot in the BigLaw firms where lawyers on the mommy track are made "of counsel" and paid part time, but often work forty or more hours a week, even if some of that is from home. That's not okay from my perspective.

If the old-school part-timer is working for herself, she probably doesn't know how to engage clients consistently, doesn't have any systems in place for client outreach and maintenance, and lacks the consistent income necessary to hire support. She ends up working full time—nights and weekends even—but again, gets paid the equivalent of a part-time worker. Not good.

The *Staffed Practice*: The *New Law Business Model* Way

When you leverage the *Staffed Practice* model the *New Law Business Model* way, it's quite fantastic.

Three-and-a-half days a week, you'll go into an actual office, where three team members are working to support you and your clients.

One of those days is focused on the business and working with the team, managing financials, and planning your marketing. The other two-and-a-half days are focused on holding Family Wealth Planning Sessions with prospects who come in pre-educated, ready to hire you, and to deliver on the plans that your team has done the heavy lifting to create.

Add in some strategic business counsel work, if you have the experience to do so, and you've got a dream practice.

Here's a closer look: As a *Staffed Practice* practicing estate planning, you might charge each client an upfront fee of $4,000. So, there you have a gross of $48,000 to $60,000 per month. And depending on efficiencies with your staff and technology, you will take home a minimum of $20,000 per month, and likely even more.

You invest the other $30,000 or so per month in your office, your team of three, marketing that turns you into the go-to lawyer in your community with just two high-converting educational presentations a month, and technology-based systems that your well-trained staff can run. These investments ensure that your clients are raving fans who pay, stay, and refer everyone they know.

While this won't happen overnight (it's our experience that the fastest this will happen is one year, and more likely eighteen months, depending on the roadblocks that will come up along your way and how you handle them), it's totally worth the time and financial investment to get there, right? With the right investments of your time, energy, attention, and money, plus the support to build it, you can build this practice model in two years or less.

Case Study: Bill

When Bill signed up for the *New Law Business Model* program, he was working for a traditional firm, doing estate planning already, but he didn't like the way the practice he was working for operated, and he didn't like his life as a lawyer at all.

Bill's billable-hours requirement had him working way more than full time. Bill didn't have any control over his life. He was married with two little kids and lived in Destin, Florida, a vacation community that he never had time to enjoy.

Bill liked the *Staffed Practice* model and thought it would be a good fit for the life he wanted to lead.

Bill left the firm he worked for, adopted the model, re-trained his staff, set up the technology systems we guided him to use, and learned how to systematically educate his community in a new way. Today, Bill hosts two high-converting *New Law Business Model* presentations every four to six weeks, bringing in, on average, twelve to sixteen pre-educated and receptive prospects each month.

This is all Bill does for marketing. No networking, no expos, no referral lunches or dinners. Bill does two presentations every six weeks and his automated systems handle the rest.

First and foremost, Bill learned to conduct the Family Wealth Planning Session we teach at the *New Law Business Model* so he gets hired by every single client he meets who needs his services, at an average fee of approximately $4,000 each.

Bill has a staff of three—a client services director, an outreach coordinator, and a file clerk—and he has a gross revenue of $600,000 to $700,000 a year. His staff, technology, and office expenses are about $400,000 annually, and he brings home around $250,000, pre-tax. (With great tax planning, he gets to keep about $200,000 of that.) Let's not forget that Bill isn't working full time at a firm—he's a *Staffed Practice.*

He works three-and-a-half days a week in his office, max.

When I asked Bill if he'd like to make a million dollars a year, he replied, "No way. I love my law practice and I love my life." He has ample free time to do whatever he wants: spend time with his family, enjoy his beautiful town, and pick up forgotten hobbies he could never have imagined pursuing while in his old job.

If Bill's life sounds too good to be true, I agree, with a caveat: it *would* be too good to be true if Bill didn't have to work for it. It'd be too good to be true if Bill hadn't needed to go way beyond his comfort zone in terms of the investments he made in the first two years of creating his own practice. But he did.

Bill's law practice is simple and streamlined and gives him the life he envisioned for himself, because he was willing to make the investments of time and money to set it up the right way from the beginning.

Bill had a clear vision that helped pull him through his fear of investing his time, energy, attention, and money, because he could see ahead to the end result of what he would create.

Along the way, whenever he got scared of the next investment or growth edge, that vision of the future gave him the courage to get him to the next step. He made a commitment and worked hard to make it happen. That, to me, is what makes it *not* too good to be true. If you decide to be a *Staffed Practice*, you'll have to work for it, too. But you can make it happen, just like Bill did. Want to hear directly from Bill about this practice model and how he did it? Join our private Facebook group, and you'll find my interview with Bill about how he did it, and you can too. You can join our Facebook group at: newlawbusinessmodel.com/awesomelawyers.

Case Study: Robert

Now, let me tell you about Robert.

Robert had been practicing law for twenty-five years, following the traditional, transactional law practice model and serving his clients in the way he was taught: keep fees as low as possible, focus on getting the documents created, send them on their way, no follow-up, find next new client ... rinse, repeat. Deadening.

This is not why Robert became a lawyer. And I don't think it's why you became a lawyer, either.

Robert had lost his love for the law. He was completely burned out, but he didn't know there was another way. He was doing what he'd always done, what he'd been educated and trained to do. He'd been doing it the same way for so long he just didn't think he had another choice.

As Robert looked ahead to the future and his retirement, he didn't feel as if his remaining years in legal practice would be any different, and he didn't see how he could use his own law practice to leave any kind of legacy to his family and community.

At some point, Robert had signed up for my email list, but he'd ignored my emails for years. Each time he saw my name in his inbox, he wondered, What could I possibly learn from this upstart woman with just a few years of legal experience?

One day, Robert changed his mind, thinking that maybe it was time to see if it was possible to teach an old dog new tricks. I don't know what made him do it on that day. Maybe he'd just hung up with an unhappy client. Maybe he'd glanced up at the dusty law school diploma framed on his wall and thought to himself, What happened to that guy? For whatever reason, Robert decided to open his mind and open my latest email.

After reading it, he found himself hitting "reply" and typing, "Okay, I'm in. Show me what to do, Ali."

Within thirty days of working with the *New Law Business*

Model, Robert increased his fees by 1,000 percent and learned to deliver his estate planning services in a new way that had him feeling totally confident that his fees were worth it. A *1,000* percent increase. And no, that's not a typo.

With a small team of three, plus his wife working by his side, Robert was able to go into his office just three days a week to serve ten to fifteen new clients per month. He was taking home more than $200,000 a year and loved his life.

Most importantly, Robert became energized by his law practice again. He no longer felt ashamed of his practice or dreaded going into the office, and instead of spending his energy looking at how he could get *out* of the law, he put his energy into building a practice he loved. Robert *loves* being a lawyer.

And the best news is, Robert just *sold* his practice for a seven-figure sum *and* he gets to keep working in the practice with a great paycheck until he decides he doesn't want to do it anymore. For now, he's an engaged and relaxed part-time lawyer with a dream home under construction, looking forward to many more years of serving clients he loves.

Is the *Staffed Practice* Model for You?

It took Bill eighteen months to go from working at a law firm full time to becoming a full-fledged *Staffed Practice*. If you look ahead eighteen months in your life and law practice, what do you see? What will you be doing day-to-day? How will you feel about your life, your law practice, and your clients? And how much time will you have for other activities, like family, friends, travel, and hobbies? Do you like where you'll be, or can you envision a better life—an ideal life working part time, loving your legal work, and earning a very healthy income?

No matter what, those eighteen months will pass you by. Are you going to look back on them with the satisfaction of having created what you want, or will you look back and see that nothing has changed?

The *Staffed Practice* is a great fit for lawyers who: want to leave the traditional, transactional way of practicing law behind; are willing to hire and train a team; and are prepared to make an up-front investment of time, energy, attention, and money in technology and other systems necessary to support growth.

We strongly recommend you do not try to reinvent the wheel here, but instead leverage already created, proven systems like done-for-you marketing, an initial consultation structure, and ongoing communication systems that are proven to work.

Meanwhile, you can download a sample pro forma

and time-blocking calendar for a *Staffed Practice* at newlawbusinessmodel.com/resources.

THE *EMPIRE BUILDER*

If the *Staffed Practice* model is so good, why wouldn't every lawyer just build that? Well, the one downside of the *Staffed Practice* model is that you are the only lawyer in the office, which means that if you want the money to keep coming in, you've got to keep bringing it in, which means that you can work three-and-a-half days a week in the office, but vacation time can be harder to come by.

Eventually, after seeing twelve to fifteen new clients a month consistently for many months, you'll start dreaming about two weeks or more out of the office, and that's where the *7-Figure Law Practice Empire Builder or 7-Figure Firm* practice model comes in.

As a seven-figure practice owner, you can take two to four weeks out of the office at a time, and still bring home $350,000 to $450,000 a year.

Building a seven-figure practice is a popular goal for lawyers, but few are able to create one with the traditional law firm model. And frankly, I don't believe most lawyers actually *want* a seven-figure law practice.

Before you set a goal of becoming a *7-Figure Firm Owner*, decide if you really want to spend most of your time focused on managing the money, the people, and the systems necessary to support your empire—rather than on seeing and serving clients. Because that's what will be necessary.

The *7-Figure Firm Owner* is needed at least four days a week in the office, more likely five days, but with the right systems in place, long vacations out of the office are possible.

The *7-Figure Firm Owner* is bringing in twenty to twenty-five new clients per month, with an average upfront fee of $4,000. We're talking $80,000 to $100,000 per month. The *7-Figure Firm Owner* is taking home a minimum of $30,000 per month, and more as she gets more efficient.

The *7-Figure Firm Owner* is investing the other $55,000 or so per month in: her office; a full-time support team of at least five, in addition to "of counsel" lawyers whom the *7-Figure Firm Owner* trains to see the clients as she shifts her focus more and more to the *business* end of the business—marketing, leadership, financials, and additional systems and marketing services that will keep her empire flush with clients.

Still with me? Good for you! Take a closer look by downloading a sample pro forma and time-blocking calendar for the *7-Figure Firm Owner* at newlawbusinessmodel.com/resources.

There are lots of reasons why my first seven-figure empire crumbled. My lack of understanding about how to handle the money part of my law practice, my failure to manage the people part of the practice, and the fact that I was constantly reinventing the wheel are just three of many reasons why it all went up in flames.

But at the core, I failed because I didn't have the *7-Figure Firm Owner* mindset.

Remember, if you are bringing in $80,000 to $100,000 per month in revenue, you are going to be writing checks in the neighborhood of $55,000 to $65,000 *per month* to pay for everything that's needed to generate that revenue consistently. That takes a mindset shift, not just a strong business structure and system.

The turning-point moment when I *really* understood that was when I was listening to a podcast with the businessman and investor Mark Cuban, and he said something like, *You build your business from where you want to be, not from where you are right now. So, look at every decision you are making and ask yourself if you are you making it as you would if you were making seven-figures.* When I did that (too late) in my own practice, I saw that by trying to scrimp on things like accounting and taxes I'd actually been sabotaging what I was trying to create.

If you want to be a *7-Figure Firm Owner*, get used to making BIG investments along the way to get there.

The 7-Figure Firm Owner The New Law Business Model Way

Building and running a *7-Figure Firm Owner* using the *New Law Business Model* (or any model, really) *is* a full-time career. But if you do it the *7-Figure* way, you do not need to work overtime to do it. And, you can definitely do it with kids. In fact, several of our lawyers have taken maternity (and paternity) leave (often more than once), while building their million-dollar law practices using the *New Law Business Model*. How? By not taking up precious time reinventing the wheel.

If you want a *7-Figure Empire*, you're going to need to leverage everywhere you can and invest your energy and emotional resources in learning how to manage your money, your team, and your time.

A practice this size comes with a hefty $600,000 to $700,000 of expenses a year. Most of that money will pay for salaries, but it will also cover your marketing, automation technology, and office expenses. Your gross monthly revenue needs to be about $100,000. You will need to engage approximately twenty to twenty-five new clients every month, at about $4,000 each.

That's a lot of new clients, and you'll burn out if you try to engage all of them yourself for too long. But you can do it sustainably, month after month, by training other of counsel attorneys to engage clients the way you want them to using our systems, and by having a solid office team and technology in place.

With this model, once you've got your team and automation systems in place, you will be spending most of your time educating your community and working *on* the business instead of *in* the business.

Case Studies: Vanessa and Darlynn

There is a wide spectrum of lawyers who have built seven-figure law practices using the *New Law Business Model*. Vanessa and Darlynn, for example, are both moms of two who took multiple maternity leaves while building their seven-figure law practices. They were able to do this with the *New Law Business Model* systems and automation.

Vanessa and Darlynn both brought in other attorneys to work in their office seeing clients, and carefully hired teams to serve their clients, leveraging technology and leadership to the max. This freed both women up to invest their time educating their communities.

They could invest energy into networking and presentations *fully* and without worrying that they were wasting any time or money, because they knew that everyone they educated who needed their services would receive proper follow-up from their teams. Every one of these prospective clients would end up on their calendars, or on the calendar of one of the attorneys they had trained. Almost without fail, when one of these prospects came in for their appointment, they would hire the lawyer. Vanessa and Darlynn both had *very* high conversion rates with very little leakage of time or energy.

Looking ahead, Vanessa and Darlynn can eventually sell their law practices for a tidy profit, if they choose to do so. In fact, Vanessa is currently in negotiations to expand from a single office into a multi-office, multi-city practice.

Case Study: David

David had been a litigator in Boston, but he was living in the suburbs and wanted to stop the dreaded commute into the city. He also only wanted to work with families. To do so, he had to learn how to engage and serve families in a completely new way. The *7-Figure Firm Owner* model appealed to David, and today, he has a thriving million-dollar-a-year-plus estate planning law practice using the *New Law Business Model* systems.

David now has another attorney in his office and several team members to support him and his clients, while he—with assistance from his wife, who has joined his firm—focuses on speaking with people in his community and building his business. David takes home $300,000 to $400,000 a year.

Yes, David is working full time, but his full-time law practice is much different from those of many lawyers with similar incomes who are constantly on the verge of burnout, working nights and weekends to get it all done. David caps his work weeks at forty hours, travels with his family regularly, and is able to plan vacations and time for himself.

He is proud of the work he does and the business he's built, and he has time for vacations and anything else he wants to do with his life.

Want to hear directly from David about the *7-Figure Firm Owner* model and how he did it? Join our private Facebook group to access my interview with David about how he did it, and you can too. You can join our Facebook group at newlawbusinessmodel.com/awesomelawyers.

Is the *7-Figure Firm Owner* Model for You?

You might love the *7-Figure Firm Owner* model if you are more entrepreneur than lawyer. Or, if you want to grow into that. You will have to become a different kind of person than you likely are right now to maintain a seven-figure law practice and life. It will likely push all of your edges around investing in yourself, growing a team, and continuing to show up for the marketing required to keep bringing in twenty to twenty-five new clients a month.

But the payoff is also worth it. When you do it right, you're building a practice you can take long vacations from, and ultimately sell, which means you'll be able to capture the full value of the many investments and sacrifices you made along the way to becoming *the* go-to lawyer in your community or industry.

HOW TO PICK THE BEST PRACTICE MODEL FOR YOURSELF

Do you have your notebook handy, the one in which you wrote your reflections, back in chapter two? Open it up and read everything you wrote about your current situation, and everything you wrote about the ideal lawyer life you envisioned.

If you haven't started the *Money Map for Lawyers* yet, do that now, too. After you've done the *Money Map*, you should have real clarity around what you want your life and law practice to look like. You'll know how many hours you want to work, how much income you want to earn, whether you want to have a team or not, and how much time, energy, attention, and money you have available to invest in growing a practice into a real business that works for you, and not the other way around.

And thanks to all that homework and soul-searching, you should have a strong feeling about which *New Law Business Practice* model sings to you.

Will you be:

- A *Solo Practitioner*, taking home around $10,000 per month, with a flexible schedule and a part-time assistant?
- A *Staffed Practice*, bringing home more than $250,000 per year, doing great work for your clients, and still finding time to pursue all those hobbies and dreams you put aside back when you started practicing law?
- Or are you shooting for the big leagues as a *7-Figure Firm Owner*, with a bustling team and a full workweek that still caps out at forty hours, and the ability to take off two to four weeks at a time?

I can't wait to find out!

Whatever you've chosen, your next step is to choose a practice area that will allow you to step into that practice model with the most ease and efficiency.

While the *New Law Business Model* was created especially for lawyers serving families or business owners, you can use it with any practice area that has clear and direct outcomes for the client, and the ability to systematize. Other practice areas for consideration include divorce mediation, bankruptcy, or worker's compensation.

WHY WE THINK ESTATE PLANNING—THE *NEW LAW* WAY—IS THE BEST PRACTICE AREA

Estate planning affects *everyone*. A significant majority of humans want to do the right thing by the people they love, who will handle their assets and children and business matters if they become incapacitated or die. And with the rise of online estate planning services, people are more educated than ever about the importance of handling these matters earlier, rather than later, in life. They are motivated to keep their families out of court. And out of conflict. On top of all that, they want to keep their affairs private and their assets out of the State Department of Unclaimed Property.

In case you're still under the impression that there are already too many estate planning lawyers out there, can I tell you something else?

Over 93 million Americans will transfer their estates in the years between 2007 and 2061. Yes, I said 93 *million*.

Ninety-two percent of those estates will be worth less than $1 million, and while you may think that this is a disadvantage to lawyers, it's not. The fact is that it's relatively easy for you to learn to serve these families in a way that is lucrative, fulfilling, and truly impactful for them. On the other hand, it's quite complex to serve families with more assets. So, you can safely bet that a large client base—certainly large enough to bring you the fifteen to twenty-five new clients a month you'll need to sustain a successful practice—awaits you if you choose to explore this option further.

One of our clients, Wendi, a long-time litigator who decided to transition into estate planning, was able to become the go-to lawyer for families in her community in just under three months, after going through the *New Law Business Model* trainings and using our materials.

Shortly after she opened her *New Law* practice, Wendi had a family come in for a Family Wealth Planning Session (the initial meeting in the *New Law Business Model*). During the meeting, she learned that the couple was shopping around, also meeting with a lawyer who'd been in practice for forty years and was the former mayor in her town.

Wendi was thrilled when the couple eventually called to say they wanted to work with her because they felt comfortable with her. They chose her because they loved how she helped them think through the hard decisions necessary for their estate planning. In other words, she had become a *relational lawyer*, as we say in the *New Law Business Model*, rather than using the traditional transactional model the more experienced lawyer was using.

Now, you might be saying to yourself, "But I hated Wills and Trusts class in law school." And, if you are, I get it.

The way that Wills and Trusts is taught in most law schools and through most CLE programs is the worst. It's transactional, not relational. It's focused on documents that we know are likely not even going to work for the families you serve. It's way overcomplicated. And, worst of all, *boring*.

When you do estate planning the *New Law Business* way, it's never boring or transactional. You will create documents, of course, but they are the byproduct of the relationship you are creating with your clients, not the thing you are selling. Instead, what you are offering your clients is a life-long trusted advisor relationship, in which estate planning documents are simply *part* of what they receive from their engagement with you.

And, if you think that those families and/or small business owners in your community won't pay for estate planning at the rates we've talked about here—on average $3,500 to $5,500 up front with ongoing payment to you ranging from $100 per year for a family with a simple situation up to $36,000 per year for high-end business owners—well, that's what most of the lawyers I knew told me when I first created this practice model over fifteen years ago.

Remember, they said families didn't want to think about

estate planning until they were old. They said families didn't want to pay the kind of rates I was talking about when they were young.

The old-school legal community said I was foolish. They said I would starve.

Instead, I built a million-dollar-a-year practice in just three years, and invented a new practice niche that many lawyers themselves use today. But here's the key, I did that by providing estate planning services that were wholly different than what most other lawyers were providing. You cannot continue to practice in the old, outdated way and expect to create a life and law practice you love.

In Part Two of the book, I'll introduce you to the Five Critical Shifts that will help you move past *your* doubts and use the *New Law Business Model* to start creating that life and law practice.

PART TWO

———

FIVE CRITICAL SHIFTS

In this section, you'll learn about some key shifts—both emotional and practical in nature—that will prepare you to practice law the *NLBM* way. I discovered these shifts after looking back at the common denominators among the most successful of our lawyers over the ten-plus years of training I did with lawyers. Each and every one of the lawyers I trained who went on to build high six- and seven-figure law practices had made these same shifts.

The first shift is to come into complete congruence—bringing your own mindset and personal affairs into alignment with the kind of practice you want to run. For example, if you're an estate planning lawyer, you'll want to do your estate plan the *New Law Business Model* way. And then talk to your family about what you did, and why—and look at how your relationships shift and grow as a result. If you're a business planning lawyer, you'll want to set up your business the *NLBM* way, with the right legal, insurance, financial, and tax foundations to support your growth. Watch what happens when you do what you are guiding your clients to do.

The second shift is to crack the time code—and when you do, you'll come to see that you are not selling your *time,* but rather an *outcome.* You'll see how you can offer that outcome in the highest quality way in the least amount of time while providing the most value to your clients. It's a breakthrough for us lawyers who have been taught to bill by the hour, or charge flat fees that are too low to actually deliver a valuable service.

The third shift is understanding and applying the affordability paradox—seeing that, yes, you *can* command premium fees and still be the most affordable solution for your clients.

You can make all of this work and become *the* go-to lawyer in your practice, no matter what community you live in, by making the fourth shift: becoming omnipresent.

Finally, you'll learn how to master all of this and transition your practice to the *New Law Business Model* by embracing mentorship, which is the fifth shift.

CHAPTER FOUR

THE FIRST SHIFT: COME INTO COMPLETE CONGRUENCE

"There are certain things that are fundamental to human ful-fillment. The essence of these needs is captured in the phrase 'to live, to love, to learn, to leave a legacy.' The need to leave a legacy is our spiritual need to have a sense of meaning, purpose, personal congruence, and contribution."

—STEPHEN COVEY

Now that you are clear from chapter one about what is and isn't working in your own life and law practice, and what your dream life and law practice could look like, it's time to get down to business around what's necessary to actually create a life and law practice you love.

I've been giving lawyers the exact scripts, templates, check-lists, and systems to transform their lives and law practices since 2006. Over that time and until the publication of this book, 2,641 lawyers have paid me for training. And, another 200,000-plus lawyers have utilized my free trainings. That's a lot of lawyers!

Some of the lawyers who have learned from me have done absolutely nothing with the training. Others have gone on to build high six- and seven-figure law practices, while taking multiple maternity (and paternity) leaves and even working part time, if they choose. And, as you read, one student (Robert) even went on to sell his law practice for a seven-figure payday.

Personally, I feel frustrated when I give a lawyer everything they need to be successful, only to see them not implement it—when I know what would happen if they did. When it came time to write this book, I decided that one of the things I wanted to give you was a clear understanding of the difference between a lawyer who creates massive suc-cess with my offerings and a lawyer who doesn't, so you can decide whether to go all in, or not.

For starters, you have to do more than just read this book. If all you had to do was read a book to experience suc-cess, then every diet book, every fitness guide, and every self-help book out there would miraculously impart life-changing wonders on any reader who took the time to plow through its chapters. You are not naïve, and I won't disrespect you with false promises. Making any dramatic life change requires more effort than that. So, exactly what will it take to make the *New Law Business Model* work for you?

I mined my own successes and failures, and those of the most successful lawyers I've worked with over the years, to identify the *Five Critical Shifts* that every lawyer who has had success with our trainings has taken on in their own life and law practice.

IT STARTS WITH CONGRUENCE

I believe that everything you see outside yourself is a reflection of your own internal consciousness. This means that you must recognize where your internal mindset and actions are out of alignment with what you claim to want.

Misalignment or lack of congruence is a hidden killer of lives and law practices. You cannot necessarily see it from the outside, which means you've got to go deep *inside* to understand if it's affecting you.

If you are out of alignment or incongruent in your life and law practice, you may have sleepless nights wondering if the work you're doing is truly meaningful. You will likely feel unfulfilled by your law practice. You will have difficulty engaging clients, even if you're using all the right words. Your networking will fall flat. You may get referrals, but they won't convert into paying clients.

The very best way I can help you to see this in your own life and law practice is to show you where and how I came to see my own incongruence and what happened when I resolved it.

MY INCONGRUENCE

I first began to see my own incongruence when I went out on my own and needed to find a new roster of clients in order to support my family. I thought getting hired would be as simple as speaking to groups in my community about the need to do estate planning. But repeatedly, the people I spoke to would respond, "Oh, I really need to take care of that," and then not call. Sometimes they would come in and meet with me for an initial consultation, but they wouldn't hire me, even though they clearly needed my services.

Over time, I learned from the best entrepreneurial and marketing geniuses how to create systems for marketing and client outreach (I'll share those systems with you in Part Three of this book). But even with those systems in place, I didn't always get great results. My cash flow was up and down (we call it the cash flow roller coaster, and I'm sure you know what I mean when I say that), inconsistent at best, nonexistent at worst. Worst of all, I was constantly worried and stressed out about not being able to pay the bills.

Why did it sometimes work out, and sometimes not? What was the secret ingredient that I sometimes left out?

I began to learn about mindset, though I really didn't know what that meant. It seemed like a buzzword that I should understand, but I really didn't.

One thing I did know was that my mindset was crap. Negative thoughts ran rampant through my mind. Thoughts like:

- *You're so stupid.*
- *You're going to run out of money.*
- *Your work isn't even valuable.*
- *You're never going to succeed.*
- *It shouldn't be this hard.*
- *You don't know what you're doing.*
- *You'll never fit in.*
- *Nobody likes you.*

On one level, I knew these thoughts weren't actually true. But that didn't stop them from causing me anxiety and even leading me into depressive funks or fits of anger that I imagine made it quite difficult for the people around me, especially my team and family.

For a long time, I thought this unkind voice in my head was something I would just have to live with, and that maybe it was, in fact, even serving me. I had convinced myself that the whole reason I had graduated first in my law school class was because of the negative thoughts that were constantly telling me how stupid I was. I believed that I'd needed those thoughts to drive me to study more than anyone else.

Looking back with the tools I have now, I can see that I could have motivated myself in a much healthier way than with constant negative self-talk.

But back then, I really didn't know that the negative thought patterns I used to keep myself moving forward were also keeping me stuck.

Stuck in my lack of gratitude, always focusing on what was wrong, instead of what was right. Stuck in my fear of rejection, seeing examples of ways I was being rejected everywhere. Stuck in my perfectionism and impossible to please.

These were just some of the ways that my craptastic mindset showed up. Despite all of this, I was having some success. But I really wasn't able to appreciate much of it.

Fortunately, I came to understand what it meant that

everything we see outside of ourselves is a reflection of our own internal consciousness. That lesson would haunt me for years, until I finally got it, and discovered how to work with it properly. I'd love to shortcut that for you here.

The first and primary way to work with this idea is to begin to notice every single place you are out of alignment, or operating without congruence. This is why we always start every lawyer who comes through *the New Law Business Model* Bootcamp training programs with a process for getting their own estate plan in place, or updated, the way that we teach. And it's why we require all of our member lawyers who are serving business owners to have their own legal, insurance, financial, and tax systems dialed-in. Only when you get your own house in order can you help others see why they need to do the same.

Here's one example of how being out of congruence impacted my ability to sign new clients, and what changed when I came into alignment.

I knew that estate planning was important, but I also knew something was off—that in the back of my mind, I was always questioning just how important it really was. Wondering about whether my services were actually valuable often kept me from being able to convey the value of estate planning to the people I met in my community.

It was no wonder that I was having trouble getting hired. I didn't really and truly believe in the service I was providing.

On top of that, I was personally stingy with my money—always looking at how I could save money, or get more for less, when hiring service providers for my own life and business.

How could I expect to command premium fees for a service I didn't fully believe in and wasn't willing to pay for when it came to my own family? Something had to shift.

MY SHIFT INTO CONGRUENCE

The only way for me to succeed—to believe in what I was doing and feel good about what I offered my clients—was to make a shift in myself to create true alignment between my life and my work.

I needed to look at any place I was asking my prospects or clients to do something I was not willing to do myself, and clean that up.

Remember the story I told you in Part I, about being out to dinner with my husband and suddenly realizing that if something happened and we never made it home to our daughter, our estate plan would fail her? That night marked the beginning of my shift into congruence—my realization that only when I could ensure that my children would be well cared for in the event of my death, would I be able to speak convincingly to my clients and community about the importance of planning.

So, I created the Kids Protection Plan for *my* family, and then began sharing about it in my community and offering it to my clients.

Then, I created a plan to track my assets (and those of my clients) properly, so nothing would be lost to the State Department of Unclaimed Property in a worst-case scenario. I also created an ongoing membership/maintenance subscription program that my clients could sign up for to keep their plans up to date.

When my own father died around that time, my most treasured inheritance from him was a ten-second voicemail he had left on my cell phone: "Lex, it's your dad. Call me back." It was the only recording I had of his voice, until the horrible day that it was accidentally deleted.

After that happened, I knew I needed to help people pass on not just their financial assets, but the intangible assets that are so often lost when someone dies. And so I began to record priceless conversations with my clients, to leave a recorded conversation for their loved ones, with their most important values, insights, stories, and experiences.

I understood that in order to convey the value of leaving this gift to one's children, I would need to create one for my own children.

Once I'd become fully congruent with my own estate planning, I was able to understand the value of the work I was doing for my clients on a whole new level. Now I could speak with them with a true understanding of their needs and desires.

I went from trying to sell estate planning documents that I kind of didn't really believe in or have confidence in, to educating, informing, and empowering the people in my community to make great decisions for themselves and the people they loved.

Once I came fully into congruence, I was able to create a system for widely educating the families in my community about the value of planning. I invited them in to meet with me for personalized support on choosing the right planning options for them, and even let them choose their own fees for my services.

I went from hours upon hours of wasted time and energy giving talks and taking meetings that didn't convert into paying clients, to having a steady stream of clients I could count on.

I no longer questioned my premium fees. I knew they were worth it. Likewise, I no longer aimed to pay as little as possible to my own service providers. I happily paid for the best services available, especially if doing so could save me time and energy—and let me relax.

I'd finally learned that any changes I wanted to make to my law practice had to be guided by deeper, more personal transformations. My practice would always show me where it needed to go, I'd discovered. To get there, I just needed to look inward, then leap.

THE MIRROR PRINCIPLE

When clients or colleagues behave in a way that you don't like, instead of blaming or thinking that you are a victim of some external force, look in the mirror.

Chances are, if you are being treated in some way that you don't like—if clients are canceling appointments, not paying on time, not taking your time seriously, for example— consider that you might be operating that same way, yourself.

For example, do you consistently have clients who are slow to pay? If so, look at whether you might be slow to pay your own bills. I noticed this one in myself. An invoice would come in from a service provider, and I'd be resistant to paying it, so I'd sit on it for a while. I'd know I was going to pay eventually, but it would take me some time to do it.

Once I realized that this behavior was causing me to experience the same thing from my own clients, I decided to make a permanent change. From then on, whenever an invoice came in, I would make myself aware of the voice in my mind saying, "You don't have the money, you're going to run out, you should wait until there's more in the bank." And then the bigger part of me, the adult part that was running the show, would respond, "It's okay, you actually do have enough. Pay the bill immediately to show the universe how you want your clients to respond to *your* bills. It will all come back to you." I would pay it immediately, no matter how much resistance I felt inside of myself.

I came to understand the "mirror principle," that everything I was doing in my own life and law practice would be reflected back to me. By choosing to operate as I wanted others to operate with me, I created the reality I wanted to experience. This was a game-changer for me because I began to see that I could not control others' behavior, but I could control my own—and that would change everything.

You may know this as the Golden Rule or the Rule of Reciprocity, but it boils down to the same thing. If you want to command premium fees, then be willing to pay premium fees. If you want people to pay for all your services up front, then be prepared to do the same. If you want people to pay on time—pay on time, or even early.

Take a few minutes right now, in your *New Law Business Model* practice journal, and write down exactly how you want to be treated by your clients. How do you want them to respect your time? How do you want them to respect your payment practices? How do you want them to show up when they meet with you? Then, look at where there may be anything incongruent with your own behavior towards others.

Also, consider where you may need the help of your own legal services. Do you need to get your own estate plan up to par? Do you need to get your own legal, insurance, financial and tax systems in place for your business so you can congruently advise your business owner clients? If so, don't just think about doing it, start by noting it in your practice journal, and then create a plan to actually do it.

Coming into complete congruence is necessary for you to successfully transition to the *New Law Business Model*. You will not be able to do presentations, network with people in your community, engage clients, or serve them in a way that you truly believe in until you make this first, critical shift.

THE MANY BENEFITS OF CONGRUENCE

If you are a criminal defense lawyer, bankruptcy lawyer,

divorce lawyer or personal injury lawyer, you can still apply a practice of congruence with what you are offering.

For example, you can choose to only represent clients who you respect and truly believe you can help. You can think of your service to them as an act of honor to yourself and to them. And you can hold a standard of only giving your clients the same advice you would give your own family and friends. Really, that is what the first critical shift is all about.

Commit to a standard of service that makes you proud. In each and every interaction, ask yourself if your way of being will increase your self-esteem, or if it will decrease your self-esteem. Only advise your clients to take the same actions you would take yourself, if you were in their shoes—regardless of the economic consequences for your practice. Know that it will all come back around. You will make all the money that you need by advising your clients with full congruence, even if this is not immediately apparent in the short term.

Invest in the trainings you need to have total confidence in your services and your ability to provide the kinds of outcomes you will be proud of. Recognize yourself as a culture creator in your community, and only deliver the kinds of legal services that you can say with confidence make the world, your clients, and your community better.

Many traditional lawyers believe that being the best means

having the most impressive law degree, having an office on the highest floor in the tallest building, being the best dressed, or having the fanciest documents and latest technology. That is *not* what your clients care about. In fact, those things can distance your prospects and clients from you. Clients are *human* and they want to feel that you are the best *human* to take care of their legal needs.

This is why, **regardless of your practice area, you can bring congruence to it through cultivating a greater relationship with your own humanity.** If you've been practicing law for a long time, you may have become jaded or cynical, and you might need some re-training on what it means to be human, and a reminder of how to bring that humanity into your law practice. Congruence is really about being the best human you can be.

Being the best human you can be, of course, has nothing to do with how big your office is—if you choose to have one—or how big your team is, or how many clients you have. Being the best human, and thus the best lawyer, that you can be comes down to connecting with your clients and understanding their needs even better than they do.

When you are fully congruent, you are able to connect with your clients not just on a mind level, but on a heart-to-heart level, so that when they meet with you they feel seen, heard, and understood more than they have with

any other professional. And when that's the case, they want to work with you, every time.

CHAPTER FIVE

THE SECOND SHIFT: CRACK THE TIME CODE

"Time is what we want most, but what we use worst."

—WILLIAM PENN

Coming into complete congruence in your life and law practice lays the foundation for what I call *cracking the time code*. This second critical shift is absolutely necessary so you can escape the outdated *transactional* legal model that leads to you working all the time, not earning enough money, and never feeling as if you can get ahead. Cracking the time code allows you to restructure how you price, package, offer and bill for your legal services, which will free up your time, give you near complete control over your calendar, let you earn all the money you want or need in the time you have, and engage with clients who are thrilled to pay for your services.

Before we dive in here, I want to remind you of something that you may take for granted. You are a lawyer! I know, it's obvious. But I'm emphasizing it because my guess is that you've forgotten just what it took for you to get here, how valuable your law degree is, and how few people make it as far as you have. In addition to discounting or downplaying all of the hard work it took to get your degree, you've probably internalized our industry's outdated billing models and overemphasis on busywork.

Bottom line: you are way undervaluing your time. Most lawyers do.

THE CATCH-22 OF TRADITIONAL BILLING MODELS

Many lawyers are still trapped by the idea that they need to bill their time in six-minute increments. Meanwhile, lawyers who have transitioned to flat-fee billing feel pressured to compete on price, often charging way too little to be able to provide great service and also be profitable.

The legal market as a whole is facing a "race to the bottom" mentality—with lawyers thinking they need to charge less and less, with a focus on price rather than on service.

As of 2019, there were 1.35 million lawyers in the United States (an increase of 200,000 in just ten years), with 40,000 new lawyers graduating law school, passing the

Bar and being sworn in each year. On top of that, at the end of 2018, venture capital investment in legal technology to automate processes previously handled by lawyers hit $1 billion. While some of this technology is focused on making lawyers' lives easier, much of it is focused on replacing lawyers with online legal document services, such as the United Kingdom's Farewell.com and, of course, LegalZoom and RocketLawyer, the two big players in the United States.

Nearly 40 percent of jobs in the legal sector could end up being automated in the long term, according to a 2016 Deloitte report. The trend toward automation is fueled by an unfortunate misalignment between the current, traditional, transactional, and hourly billing models and the real needs and resources of everyday people seeking legal help. Hourly billing models incentivize you, the lawyer, to keep cases going as long as possible, bill as many hours as possible, and, frankly, continue to be inefficient. And your clients are incentivized to communicate as little as possible, do as much themselves as they can, and often make costly mistakes along the way. It's a lose-lose, a Catch-22.

While online legal service providers can certainly benefit people who couldn't afford legal services in the past, they spell trouble for you unless you up-level your services beyond those that a robot could perform.

In order to survive and thrive and serve your clients in the highest and best way possible, you must completely shift the way you think about your time and income. Whether you're billing hourly or creating low-priced, flat-fee package services, these traditional transactional models make it incredibly difficult for you to earn a decent living or provide quality services to your clients.

THE SECRET YOU NEED TO KNOW

In this chapter, I will show you how to shift the way you think about the services you provide so you no longer need to compete on price and are incentivized to provide the best service to your clients in the shortest amount of time, which is best for them and for you.

Once you know this code-cracking secret, you'll be able to *increase the value of the outcome you provide* to the clients you are serving, regardless of the hours you spend working. You will learn to provide that value as efficiently as possible, to everyone's benefit. Let's look at what I mean.

CASE STUDY: ADAM—FROM HOURLY BILLING TO HIGH-VALUE OUTCOME

Adam was a typical private practice lawyer, charging $250 an hour. He wanted to bill out all his time, collect all his fees, and make $20,000 a month. For that to happen, he would have to bill eighty hours a month—just twenty hours each week. Sounds easy, right?

When you work for a BigLaw firm, you can bill twice that—forty hours a week for fifty weeks, or 2,000 hours a year. This is possible because that BigLaw firm has a lot of people and systems in place to support you. You don't have to put time into networking, or meeting with prospects who don't hire you, or any of the other time-consuming things that you must do as the owner of your own law practice to generate business. In a typical BigLaw job, you don't do your own administrative tasks, either. You get fed legal work and get paid to do that legal work, and you can do that all day every day, billing for most of the hours you are actually working.

Contrast that with running your own practice, like Adam was. To bill eighty hours a month, you may have to work sixty to eighty hours a week, because you have to do all the tasks that a firm typically provides for their lawyers. First, you have to find the clients; then you have to get them to call; then you have to handle your intake well so you get hired; then you have to do all the admin associated with marketing and engagement. Then, of course, you have to actually deliver on the service. Oh, and don't forget technology setup and maintenance! And invoicing! And, of course, you'll need continuing education, not just on the law, but also on how to run a business, because it's all on you now. Then there's hiring and firing—you'll need to leave time for that.

Oh jeez Louise, I'm exhausted just writing about all of this.

It's no wonder Adam was stressed to the max before he came to my team and me for help. He never knew where the next new client would come from, took whatever business came through his door, constantly felt behind and sub-par, worked nights and weekends and *still* struggled to make enough money. He felt as if he was in over his head because he *was*.

With the *New Law Business Model*, Adam stopped taking whatever business walked in the door. He focused exclusively on educating and serving families and small business owners who valued his time and expertise.

Adam stopped billing by the hour (unless required to do so by the court), and even by the number of documents he produced. He also took control of his time by limiting his firm's court matters to those that had to do with the incapacity or passing of a client; and he was able to outsource his court appearances on those matters nearly completely.

After Adam switched from accepting any client who walked in the door and charging $250 an hour—working like a crazy person, having inconsistent up-and-down income from one month to the next (we call this the cash flow roller coaster)—and learned to implement the *New Law Business Model*, his entire life changed. With technology and outsourcing support, he was able to provide excellent service while earning $4,000 per client for an average of five hours of work per client. This is what we call cracking the time code.

In the traditional model, only the most senior law firm partners at the biggest law firms could command fees of $1,000 or more per hour. But now, any lawyer who is prepared to learn a new way of educating and serving their community can effectively do the same.

Now, keep in mind, that with the *New Law Business Model*, you would never be charging a client $1,000 an hour for legal services. In fact, there is no hourly billing at all. Everything you do is flat-fee, agreed to in advance, so there are never any surprises. This is one of the brand promises that *New Law Business Model* lawyers make to their clients. The clients you serve aren't paying for your hours, they are paying for *your high-value outcome* for their family or business, and the confidence with which you can create that for a single flat fee (or ongoing strategic service), which they actually *choose* for themselves. *Now* we have a win-win: you are incentivized to be efficient and they are happy to pay your fees. In order to crack the time code, Adam needed to confidently deliver a high-value service with an outcome that the people in his community would be happy to pay for, and then share the benefits of that service with his community.

Adam did just that by learning to provide relational legal services that created a experience for his clients, turning them into raving fans who referred all of their friends, family, clients, and colleagues to him. Importantly, Adam invested in the training and technology he needed to leverage his time and energy efficiently.

Yes, in order to crack the time code in his own life and law practice, Adam had to make investments beyond law school. He had to learn a new way to serve his clients and educate his community. Then he needed to invest in the team and technology to serve his clients. But his law practice will be paying him back for those investments forever—especially when and if he one day decides to sell the business.

To crack the time code, we as lawyers must break free of our old, outdated modes of thinking of ourselves as people who trade our time, minute by minute, for money. Instead, we must start to think of ourselves as entrepreneurs and business owners, who invest in the systems that support us best.

I believe the foundation for a successful law practice and a peaceful life is knowing you have enough money coming in *and* enough time to enjoy it. Managing your time and money empowers you to intentionally create the life you want.

WHERE TO FOCUS YOUR TIME, ENERGY, ATTENTION AND MONEY (TEAM) RESOURCES

"If your business depends on you, you don't own a business—you have a job. And it's the worst job in the world because you're working for a lunatic!"

—MICHAEL E. GERBER, *THE E-MYTH REVISITED*

Many lawyers follow a strategy laid out in the book *Profit First* by Michael Michalowicz. This approach is based on the premise of: *Look, you're a business owner and you'll never learn to look at your numbers, so just do it this way: take 10 or 15 percent off the top to pay yourself first; then take some out for taxes; and then run your business with whatever is left.*

That could be a good model for business owners who aren't willing or able to learn how to be smart businesspeople, or perhaps in the beginning stages of business. However, if you run your business according to the *Profit First* model, your options for making smart investment choices and business decisions are limited. Why limit yourself? You're a lawyer. You're very, very smart. And with guidance and support, you can learn to be a smart businessperson too.

The first step is to learn where to focus your time, energy, attention, and money.

I believe most worry, stress, and strain comes from not knowing if you're doing the right thing on a moment-to-moment, day-to-day, week-to-week, and month-to-month basis. **When you know you're doing the right thing every day to reach your goals, and you have a clear view of the outcome, your nervous system can relax.** Sometimes, what needs to be done is hard work, but as a lawyer, you're used to hard work. Hard work isn't your problem. **Knowing what to do and where to focus your attention is the problem.**

FIVE KEY METRICS

If you've been following along, you probably already know how many clients you need to engage each month, and the average fee you need to charge to hit your financial goals. If you don't know this yet, go to moneymapforlawyers.com and go through the free program there so you have the clarity you need to use your law degree to meet your personal financial and life goals.

With this information in mind (and you should have this written in your notebook from chapter two) you are able to track just five key metrics each month to know whether you are on track to reach your goals, and stay focused on what you need to fix, if you are not meeting your goals.

Here are the five key metrics to track:

1. How many inquires do I receive each month?
2. How many of these inquiries turned into booked appointments?
3. How many of those appointments were kept?
4. How many of those kept appointments turned into paying clients?
5. At what average fee?

If you look at just these five items every single week, you'll begin to identify where to focus your time, energy, attention, and money, instead of spinning your wheels wasting time, energy, attention, and money.

TIME AND MONEY MENTORING WITH THE *NLBM*

When you create a cash flow forecast plan for your law practice, monitor the five metrics you need to focus on, and use a time-blocking calendar to manage your time, everything lines up. Then you can truly relax and know you're on track to reach your goals.

Your ideal outcome is learning where to invest your resources, which extend far beyond just money. Your resources are your time, energy, attention, and money (TEAM resources), and they all need to be allocated properly. When you learn to allocate your TEAM resources well, creating the life and practice you want becomes much less stressful and a heck of a lot easier.

The very first thing our coaches at the *New Law Business Model* do once a lawyer joins us as a member is to create a cash forecast and time-blocking calendar to ensure our member lawyer's life and law practice goals line up.

You can do this for yourself by using the resources at moneymapforlawyers.com as a starting place.

By knowing what your financial and time goals are, seeing clearly how many clients you need to engage at what average fee, blocking your time to reach and serve those clients, and then looking at the right metrics to properly diagnose where you need to focus your attention, you will be able to crack the time code in your own law practice.

CHAPTER SIX

THE THIRD SHIFT: LEVERAGE THE AFFORDABILITY PARADOX

Cracking the time code entails charging fees that are high enough to allow you to take the time necessary to provide quality service that you believe in. Knowing that you, quite nobly, want to be an affordable solution for your clients, I found a way for you to deliver truly meaningful and impactful services while also saving your clients money. At the *New Law Business Model,* we call this the "affordability paradox," and you need to understand it in order to be affordable and accessible to your clients without sacrificing your personal life or the quality of your services.

If you focus on being the cheapest option, you simply

can't deliver the kind of service that truly benefits your clients, and you certainly can't do it at rates that are sustainable for your life and law practice. If you focus on providing cheap services, you will need to see more clients and deliver a lower quality of service in order to make enough to survive. Fortunately, when you understand the affordability paradox, you can charge premium fees and still be the most affordable solution for your clients.

YES, I SAID, "AFFORDABLE PREMIUM FEES."

It may seem paradoxical to be able to charge premium fees and still be the most affordable solution for your clients. That's why we call it the affordability paradox. And when you understand and leverage it, you can confidently charge premium fees for the high value outcome you provide. By leveraging the affordability paradox, you can command the fees you need, have the life you want, and deliver the highest quality service. It also benefits your clients with the highest and best outcomes. And yet—*ta-da!*—you're *still* the most affordable solution for your clients' needs.

Educating your clients to make informed and empowered choices when it comes to hiring you is the imperative here. Otherwise, your clients have no basis other than pricing to make a decision about whether to plan with you or the guy down the street.

I figured this one out the hard way when I was once hired by a client for a $5,500 fee, only to have them cancel two weeks later when they thought they'd found the same plan for just $2,500. I almost threw in the towel on my law practice then and there.

From this painful (and expensive) experience, I saw that clients had no way to choose among their different planning options other than based on price, and that it was my job to guide them to understand the various options and the impact of their choices.

So, I didn't throw in the towel. Instead I doubled down and hired consultants to help me, because I definitely couldn't figure it out alone. I had already spent hours upon hours learning from other lawyers how to quote my fees, and I clearly wasn't doing it right.

HOW THE FAMILY WEALTH PLANNING SESSION MAKES AFFORDABLE PREMIUM FEES POSSIBLE

So I asked for help, and got it—for a $20,000 investment with the best consultants I could find on pricing and packaging of professional services. On the advice of my consultants, I stopped offering a free meet and greet consultation and instead created the Family Wealth Planning Session, an initial meeting structure and fee quoting system that is now at the heart of the *New Law Business Model*. The

Family Wealth Planning Session guides prospects to understand their planning options and choose their own fee, at the intersection of the outcomes they want for their family and the budget they have to pay for planning.

The very first time I used the Family Wealth Planning Session, it paid off! After forty-five minutes together, my prospective client told me he was ready to move forward; then and there in my office, he chose his fee, we designed his plan, signed the engagement letter and I collected payment. I was elated. Prior to that, I had often spent up to four hours with prospects, only to hear, "I have to think about it" or "We'll need to get back to you." Which they wouldn't.

When you know exactly what to say and how to say it in an initial client meeting so the prospective client feels confident and in control, you've leveraged the affordability paradox to everyone's advantage.

HOW IT WORKS

Being able to charge affordable premium fees begins with an effective intake process that educates your prospects before they ever book an appointment to meet with you. Your intake process should involve some education that properly prepares your prospect for their initial meeting with you.

This preparation could be a short phone conversation with

you or your intake team member. Some of our lawyers even require their prospects to attend an educational presentation before coming in to meet with them for the first time. Of course, if you do require a presentation first, you need to make sure the presentation is so good that it will convert the listeners into booked appointments on your calendar. Otherwise, they get educated by you and hire someone else. We call this marketing for your competition, and you definitely don't want to do that!

Once your intake process has properly qualified your prospect and they have decided to book an initial meeting with you, they must complete pre-meeting homework. This homework will begin to help them even before they've hired you, immediately establishing you as a trusted advisor. It will also help you to help them to make wise choices during the initial meeting.

As for the initial meeting itself, it's not your typical meet and greet or "free initial consultation." Rather, it's a valuable working session that has a name, a purpose and a value. And, it does need to be valuable.

This is why our Personal Family Lawyer members (these are lawyers who have been trained in the *New Law Business Model* way of serving families and are licensed to use our resources in their own practices) call their initial meeting a Family Wealth Planning Session. The name cements the meeting's purpose: to create a plan that will bring wealth to the people they love.

This meeting is not a free consultation, but instead a $750 meeting, which prospects can have at no charge if they commit to doing the homework and submitting it ahead of time. However, if they do not want to submit homework ahead of time, they can pay for the meeting and the Personal Family Lawyer will do the homework with them during the meeting.

We have a similar structure for lawyers working with business owner clients. And, we've supported lawyers to create similar structures in their personal injury, bankruptcy, divorce, and immigration practices. The key here is that there is a system, a structure, pre-education, and clear boundaries. Your prospects don't just get to schedule with you at any time, at no charge, and with no pre-work on their part up front.

Once the pre-educated and prepared prospect comes in, they are taken through a working session focused on whether they need your services. The prospect is also helped to understand the downfalls of lesser plans. Once they choose *your* plan, they are supported to choose a fee that matches their budget and desired outcome.

Using this structure, our Personal Family Lawyer and

Family Business Lawyer members often have a 100 percent engagement rate, at average fees in the $4,000 range. How can they command such high fees when people can go online and do estate planning for under $150 or hire another lawyer in their town for $1,200 to prepare a will and trust? Because our members have learned to communicate to their prospects why it's actually more affordable for them and their family to pay more. As a result, our lawyer members are able to provide a superior service and meet their personal financial and time goals. They can map out exactly how many two-hour Family Wealth Planning Sessions they need to have each month to meet those goals.

Offering a flat-fee packaged service and, where appropriate, recurring "affordable premium" services, will be the key to your happiness as a lawyer, truly.

CAN THIS WORK IN YOUR COMMUNITY?

You might legitimately be wondering if affordable premium fees can work in your community. The answer is yes. Here are three case studies that illustrate how the affordable premium model works in various sized communities across the United States.

REVISITING ROBERT

Let's return to Robert, the *Staffed Practice* who sold his practice for a seven-figure payday. Before Robert understood the affordability paradox, he was charging just $400 for a will package because he wanted his services to be affordable. Robert felt that he had to charge that little, because he was competing with other lawyers in town who were charging just a few hundred dollars for a will, and of course, he was also competing with online legal services.

Let's look, though, at the results of that $400 will package. What was the true outcome Robert was delivering to his clients? With a $400 will, Robert was virtually guaranteeing that his clients' families would end up in court in the event of their incapacity or death. So while it may have seemed to Robert's clients that they were saving money by paying just $400 for a will package, they weren't taking into account the cost on their families, after it would be too late.

When Robert put the Family Wealth Planning Session process in place in his law practice, his average fee increased by 1000 percent, from $400 for a will package to $4,000 for a comprehensive plan.

He generated $48,000 in new business in the first sixty days. But, of course, that was just the beginning, because once Robert knew how to do this, he was able to shift his entire relationship to his law practice. He went on to create a multi-six-figure law practice working just three days a week in his office. Best of all, within ten years, Robert sold his law practice for a seven-figure payout. In the end, Robert could serve fewer clients and *command affordable premium fees by guiding his clients to see that paying more during life would actually be the most affordable solution for their family.*

If that sounds too good to be true, it's not. I encourage you to hear Robert tell you why, himself, at newlawbusinessmodel. com/resources. By truly helping his clients make the wisest choices for the people they loved, leveraging the affordability paradox and an educational process that his community loved, Robert transformed his life and law practice from a dead-end career that he'd have to work at until he died to a business he was excited about and could sell for a profit in order to retire on his timeline.

REVISITING BILL

Bill, from chapter three, is another perfect example of how leveraging the affordability paradox works in any market. As a *Staffed Practice,* Bill serves families in the small vacation town of Destin, Florida. The population is just 13,312 and the median household income is $68,078.

Recall that Bill, after an eighteen-month transition to the *New Law Business Model,* is now able to spend just three-and-a-half days a week in his office, and consistently serve twelve to fifteen new clients a month at an average fee of $4,000. Bill now brings in $600,000 to $700,000 a year gross, taking home $200,000 to $250,000 annually by providing affordable premium legal services to clients who truly care about their families and want to keep them out of conflict and court.

Bill is able to do this because he has learned how to educate his community in a new way. He knows how to provide a plan to clients that is different—and far superior to—what they could find online or from another attorney who charges less. Bill does charge higher rates, but for truly affordable solutions that provide the best outcomes for his clients, and most importantly Bill knows how to inform, educate and empower his community, prospects and clients. We'll check in with Bill again in the next chapter and see how he helps his neighbors in Destin make the best choices for the people they love.

CASE STUDY: BOB

Bob also lives in a small town of just 11,596 people, in Massachusetts. The median family income in Bob's town is higher than Bill's at $95,864. Within sixty days of working with the *New Law Business Model,* Bob raised his fees from $300 to $500 for simple wills to an average of $4,500.

CASE STUDY: SUE

Finally, let's take a look at Sue, a lawyer who lives in Greensboro, North Carolina. Greensboro has a population of 269,999, which is substantially bigger than Bob's or Bill's towns, yet the median household income is only $41,628. Even though they're not millionaires, the families in Sue's community would rather pay premium fees for a plan done well than risk having their families end up in court or conflict. These families are Sue's neighbors, colleagues, and friends, and they're thrilled that Sue is their trusted advisor. Sue has become the go-to lawyer for families in her community.

HOW CAN YOU COMPETE WITH CHEAP ONLINE SERVICES?

The answer is, you can't, nor should you try. You simply cannot deliver meaningful services to clients at the price that cheap online services can. And cheap online services cannot provide the value that you can, when you've got a true understanding of the services you can provide to your clients and the support you can offer to help them achieve their desired goals and outcomes. When you really realize the value of the outcomes you provide, you'll never think you need to compete with cheap online services, or even lawyers who aren't charging enough, again. Instead, you need to focus on providing affordable premium services that allow you to provide the high-value outcome your clients want but cannot get online.

Technology will not put you out of business. In fact, technology can help you once you learn how to leverage it to make your business even better. For example, I use technology to provide free legal documents to clients and prospective clients. I give away guardian nomination documents, automated webinars, and ongoing education to people who need my help and want to benefit from the affordable premium services I provide.

Not every potential client needs me, and not everyone will need you. Some people really do just want a cheap legal document. Some people don't prioritize keeping their families out of court and conflict. Some business owners don't prioritize setting up their business with premium legal, insurance, financial, and tax systems. Guess what? Those aren't your clients. Ferret them out using your system so you can focus on those who *are* your clients—the people who *do* care.

CHAPTER SEVEN

THE FOURTH SHIFT: BECOME OMNIPRESENT

The old way of marketing can feel quite a lot like a merry-go-round. It's why we call it the marketing merry-go-round. You get on it with a hope, a wing, and a prayer, not really sure what you're doing. The ride typically starts with you getting out into the community to do some networking. But very quickly, you realize your networking is not working.

So, you decide you'll invest a little more in developing referral sources beyond just plain old networking. You start doing some breakfasts and lunches with people who might be able to send you business. But now, instead of getting business, you're getting fat.

You think, *Hmm, maybe I should go out and do presentations.*

So you go to a networking event, perhaps a small business owners' group, where you give a fifteen-minute talk on business planning. You pass around your business cards and everyone tells you how wonderful your talk was. Many of them say that what you have to offer is exactly what they need. You drive home, buoyed by your success. How many business owners and entrepreneurs were there in the room? Thirty? Forty? Surely this day will pay off with enough clients to keep you gainfully employed for months!

Here's what really happens. Those business cards end up tucked into wallets and dropped into purses. They get thrown into the back seat, with all the other paperwork, or placed on a desk as a "when I get some time" item for follow-up. That time never comes. Those people who were so excited by your talk will probably never look at your card again. While they left your talk educated, it's very likely that you were marketing for your competition, because by the time they are ready to hire someone, they will have long forgotten your name.

Then one day as you're sitting by the phone, waiting for it to ring as you surf social media for prospects, you get a call from a local magazine inviting you to run an ad. They flatter you, and it feels good, so you go for it. Only to get no results.

Maybe you've even resorted to paying for leads, but those leads haven't turned into paying clients, either.

You've been burned so many times that you're understandably hesitant to invest in marketing again. You don't know what to do, so you do nothing, frozen in analysis paralysis.

Or, perhaps you do figure out something that works, but it takes a lot to do it consistently, especially once you get busy. So you do the thing that works until your calendar gets full, and then you stop doing the thing that works, finish the client work you took on, look up and realize you're starting at zero again.

The marketing merry-go-round. It's enough to make you sick—maybe so sick that you give up and stop doing any marketing at all.

Are you nodding your head? Is this you? Don't feel bad. This is how it is for most professional practice owners—not just lawyers. Because no one's ever taught us how to do it right.

MY MISADVENTURES IN MARKETING

Like so many lawyers, I knew nothing at all about marketing when I first started my own law practice, and I was shocked by how much there was to learn and how costly it would be to learn it.

When I first left the BigLaw firm to start my own business, I thought I'd fairly easily get four to six new clients a month at an average of $3,000, and that would replace my old salary of $180,000 a year. It seemed easy enough, and so I started going out into my community and talking to a lot of people. I networked like crazy, going to lunches, giving talks and presentations, and telling anyone who would listen about what I had to offer. Most of these people seemed excited to meet me and would say things like, "Wow, thank you so much. That was so great. I need to do that." But that was it. They never called.

Why weren't they calling me? After a while—a short while—I started worrying a little bit, then I actually got scared. I didn't have any sort of financial cushion to fall back on if I couldn't make a go of my own business. And I didn't have money to invest in marketing, just time, which I didn't know how to optimize very well.

In law school, I wasn't taught how to engage clients, and neither were the vast majority of lawyers I've spoken to over the years. We came into this field with the assumption that once we had the education, the law degree, and the valuable skills, people would flock to us, begging for our services. But that's not how it works with legal practices, or with any business, for that matter.

INTENTIONAL MARKETING

Fortunately, you can make the shift to becoming omnipresent in your community without having to go to every networking event, coffee, and lunch you're invited to (which you do not have the time for). How? It starts with systematically and strategically shifting from the old way of marketing to a whole new way.

The new way of marketing begins with a clear intention, which means you know who you serve, why you serve them, and how to educate them. Then you can create a systematic plan for doing so that gets you in front of your ideal clients consistently, with as much automation and as little of your personal time as possible.

First and foremost, this means you must stop taking on every client who walks in the door because you think you have to in order to pay the bills. We call this being a "door lawyer," and it's the fastest path to your own law practice misery.

Think of it this way: if you take whoever walks in the door, you can never create systems to become highly efficient, because you have to reinvent the wheel and learn an entirely new practice area for each new client. You can never truly feel confident with your services, because you're always in learning mode. Finally, you can never become known as *the* go-to lawyer in your community, because you're not.

So, the first step to getting intentional with your marketing is to choose a specific practice area that you want to become the expert in, and then to choose a specific group of people who you want to serve within that practice area.

This is an easy, three-step process:

1. Start by identifying who you would love to serve.
2. Then, determine the outcomes that you would love to provide.
3. Next, design your services and an education plan for your market.

If you're afraid that by narrowing down your client base you'll be restricting your growth, I get it. I had that fear, too. Yet, so long as you choose to serve a market of people who truly do need your services, and you've run the numbers to ensure there really are plenty of them to serve, then your fear is not based in reality. You're operating with a scarcity mindset, not a reality mindset. Now that you've realized this, it's time to shift that mindset—fast.

As I told you at the beginning of this book, when I first decided to focus on serving families with minor kids in my community, every lawyer I told about it said I would starve. They said young families didn't want to think about estate planning, and they definitely wouldn't pay well for it. But I knew they were wrong, because *I* was a young mom and I would pay anything to do the right thing for my kids.

Once I was willing to get intentional with my marketing and become omnipresent in my community, focusing on the needs of families with minor children, my dream came true: I became the go-to lawyer for young families in my community.

And here was the coolest part, which I didn't anticipate. Once I focused my intentional marketing on families with young children, I started getting inquiries from many other types of clients as well—small business owners, the elderly, and high-net-worth grandparents.

Suddenly, my intentional marketing was bringing in a much wider range of prospects than I would have called in if I had tried to reach all of those markets directly. Once I mastered my first avatar (families with young children), I created specialized services that business owners and retirees wanted, and expanded my practice to serving them, as well.

WHERE TO SOURCE REFERRALS

The next thing to shift your mindset on is how you work with referral sources. The most important thing to know here is that it's about quality, not quantity. In my early years of practice, I thought I needed to have loads of referral sources, and it turned out that was a waste of my energy. You actually need fewer referral sources than you think. Eventually, I learned to focus on cultivating and educating only three high-quality referral sources for my ideal clients.

Your best referral sources are people who serve your ideal client with complimentary services. And think outside the box here.

Of course, estate planning lawyers all know that financial advisors and insurance agents are good referral sources, but my best referral sources were Mommy and Me group leaders, lactation consultants, and even a 3-D imaging fetal ultrasound company. I would cultivate relationships with my referral sources in a formalized setting, such as by hosting a regular study group or organizing a joint marketing campaign for our mutual client base. Then I would ask them to send me any clients in need of estate planning services, and to copy me on the email or text, so I could immediately begin educating the referral about my services.

Most importantly of all though, when it came to my referral sources, is that I properly educated them about how I was different than most lawyers, so they weren't sending me clients who were expecting to get cheap documents, as they would from other lawyers. And, I quickly realized I didn't really need that many referral sources—three to five great ones could keep my practice busy enough to meet my goals.

START WITH FREE MARKETING

Free marketing is basically effective networking that actually works. This does not include random luncheons and dinners where you have no idea who will be there, or whether or not they need or will be willing to pay for your services. Free marketing does involve educating your referral sources, and speaking to affinity groups and attending expos and trade shows where your market is. To do it effectively, you also need to develop your automated personalized follow-up systems. This is critical so please do not overlook it, otherwise your free marketing will fall flat and you'll think it doesn't work. But, with the right follow-up systems in place, it absolutely does.

Until you've got your client engagement system (intake process, initial meeting process, fee quoting system) dialed in to the point where you're getting hired by at least 80 percent of the people you meet with, you want to only engage in free marketing. This is not really free, of course, because it costs you time. Once you understand how to maximize every drop of your time, it will be more valuable to you than money. You can always make more money, but you cannot make more time.

SPEAKING TO AFFINITY GROUPS

One of the most effective strategies for free, intentional marketing is to speak to relevant groups in your community. For me, this meant conducting lunch-and-learn sessions at tech offices and other law firms as well as educating members of parents' clubs, community service organizations, real estate brokers, CPAs, and churches with young family bases. I learned to make sure that every speaking engagement translated into at least one booked initial consultation.

For a detailed resource on how to use speaking presentations to generate clients (and not just rave reviews), visit http://newlawbusinessmodel.com/resources.

Again, you'll want to develop your personalized automation systems so you are able to effectively follow up with everyone you meet at your speaking engagements. If you do not have an effective system for following up with the people you meet through your free marketing, you'll be leaving huge amounts of income and impact on the table.

FOLLOWING-UP AND STAYING IN TOUCH

Typically, someone needs to be exposed to you and your message about a dozen times before they are ready to make a hiring decision. This is what builds the know, like, and trust factor that results in you getting hired. Most lawyers are afraid to follow up even once or don't have the systems for it. So, if you've got a system to help you make consistent, weekly contact with the people you meet, you're going to stand out from the crowd in a way that truly matters. And, yes, you can automate all of it to make it very efficient and effective.

Thanks to my personalized automation systems, I was able

early on to stay top of mind with 5,000 people in my community on a regular basis. Most lawyers aren't willing to do that, they think it's annoying. What they don't realize is that it's only annoying to people who aren't interested in their services, or if they are sending out uninteresting legal content.

And while only about 15 percent of the 5,000 people on my email list opened any given email I sent, that was still more than 600 people reading my messages regularly.

The content I sent out was personal and engaging, once I learned how to do it. I would regularly have people come to my office after years of receiving my email newsletters and say, "Wow, Ali, it's so good to meet you. I've been getting your emails for so long I feel as if I know you."

That's the key to effective networking. It's all in the follow-up.

There is so much going on in people's lives, so many demands vying for their attention, that you have to find a way to rise above the noise. One way to do this is by offering something to everyone in the room at a speaking engagement—something you know they want and need—with the caveat that they have to provide you with their email address and phone number (at minimum), and ideally their physical address as well, so you can send them the free thing you offered as follow-up. Now, you are in control of the relationship going forward.

For example, after each networking event, you might send everyone you met an immediate email with a digital gift, or even better a handwritten note with a non-digital gift. Our Personal Family Lawyer members use my book *Wear Clean Underwear: A Fast, Fun, Friendly—and Essential—Guide to Legal Planning* for follow-up.

That kind of personalized follow-up is easy, using an automated system. Here's how it might work. Immediately after the event, you enter the names and contact info of each person who attended into your database (or better yet, you have a team member who does that). Ideally, your automation system then triggers a series of events that you do not have to monitor.

You or your team member immediately follow up with a phone call to each person, confirming their contact info and reminding them that you'll be sending them the thing you promised. Ideally, the call should not come from you, but from an outsourced (or in-house) team member you've hired to manage calls and appointments. The caller should contact each person and say something like, "Hi, it's Susan calling on behalf of Ali Katz, who you just met at such-and-such event. I'm going to send you the gift she promised, and I want you to know I'm here in case you have any questions."

Then, once you've sent out the requested thing, you put that person on your automated nurture sequence and weekly email newsletter campaign. Eventually, as your automation system grows, you'll be posting the same content you send out via email to your social media sites, and on your own website. You may think that you only need to use one platform, and that posting the same content on social media that you send in your newsletter is overkill or unnecessary, but actually it's the exact thing that will make you omnipresent. Even if a prospect only reads your content in one place, the fact that they see you everywhere creates trust.

Setting up this type of automated marketing system does require an investment of time, energy, attention and money, but if you do it step-by-step and remember that you're playing a long game (building a law practice is a marathon, not a sprint), it will pay off for you.

If you have not already, check out the all-in-one, automated practice management system my partner and I created for lawyers at newlawbusinessmodel.com/resources.

Building the systems you need to become omnipresent in your community is truly the best investment you can make, because it's what leads you to having consistent, steady, predictable revenue you can count on serving clients you love. And that's truly the holy grail, in my book.

PAID MARKETING

Once you know how to get hired by every person you meet with who needs your services, and you've got your automated follow-up systems in place, it's time to start paying for your marketing.

Warning: do *not* invest in any type of paid marketing—not buying leads, not ads, not social media, *nothing*—until you have an intake and engagement process that results in you getting hired and paid by at least 80 percent of the people you talk to who need your services. Until you have that in place, you *must* focus your efforts on getting that dialed in. Once that's dialed in, go crazy on the paid marketing. Now you know it will pay off.

So, what kind of paid marketing should you be doing? Any and all that it takes to get your calendar booked with exactly the right number of initial consults each month to meet your personal, financial, and time goals.

Before we delve into your options, it's critical to know exactly how many clients you need to engage each month (and at what average fee), so you can create your time-blocking calendar and have only as many initial consultations available (at specific times and dates) as you need. If you have not already completed your *Money Map for Lawyers* to get clear on how many clients you need each month, and at what average fee, go back and do that before you start your paid marketing.

Most of the lawyers we serve who are implementing the *New Law Business Model* in their practices find themselves full, and booked out four to six weeks in advance, providing them with a huge amount of assurance and security, while also giving them full control of their calendars.

We have found that the most streamlined and efficient use of paid marketing is to drive people to educational resources and eventually to an educational presentation that leads to an initial consult with you.

Most of our lawyers are hosting between two and six presentations per month (online and offline) to educate the people in their community, and their paid marketing is focused on getting people to attend those presentations.

The benefit of using paid marketing in this way is that your presentation is specifically designed to result in educated prospects who book appointments with you, and for anyone who is not quite ready to hire you, to get put on a long-term nurture/follow-up (or as we call it consistent communication) campaign so they will hire you when they're ready. Or, refer you to any friends, family, clients and colleagues who do need your services.

Yes, you can do paid marketing that is specifically focused on running ads, or even billboards, TV, and radio. But if that paid marketing is just directing people to call your office, you're losing a huge amount of the money you're investing in that paid marketing because most people who see or hear your ads aren't educated enough to know they need to call your office. And if they don't call your office (because they aren't ready when they see your ad), you have no way to build a relationship with them and stay top of mind.

Instead, if your ad sends them to a page that gives away free education, then they can exchange their contact information for that resource, and you can build a relationship with them until they are ready to hire you. By doing it this way, you make the most of your paid marketing dollars.

CASE STUDY: DEBRA

Debra is a single mom who was doing litigation work and realized that she could not provide the kind of attention her daughter needed if she did not have full control over her schedule. So she came to us to transition into estate planning, serving families in her community in a new way.

Once she learned how to do estate planning the way we teach, created her own plan to serve four to six families a month, and completed two practice plans using our Family Wealth Planning Session intake and engagement system, Debra was ready to start her free marketing.

Debra leveraged our educational resources and client

referral system to serve families with young children in her community. She didn't have to create any of the materials or systems. She only needed to learn how to use them.

Debra didn't want to spend any money on marketing right away (remember, while you're learning to engage clients, you want to take advantage of free marketing) so she started by contacting private schools in her community about donating a silent auction basket. These silent auction baskets, which are a resource provided by the *New Law Business Model*, can be used in a fundraiser or to build relationships with private schools. Families with young children who are in a private school are typically a good market for estate planning, because they have great concern for their children's well-being and, once educated about why an estate plan is necessary, are willing and able to pay for one for their family.

As a result of Debra's donation to the silent auction, she was asked to speak to the employees at a local company. Using a presentation we provided her with, Debra was able to educate the thirty-two people in attendance. Twenty of them made appointments with her for a Family Wealth Planning Session. Out of those twenty people, sixteen hired Debra at an average fee of $3,500.

I'll do the math for you: that's $56,000 that Debra earned

from her free marketing. Best of all, the company wants Debra to return and offer her presentation every six months.

Debra could base her entire marketing strategy on visiting corporations and giving presentations. The key is, she knows that every person she sits down with who needs her services will hire her because she's armed with the right resources and has invested six months' time ramping up and learning exactly how to make that happen.

CASE STUDY: BILL

Contrast Debra's story with that of Bill, the *Staffed Practice* who set out two years ago to grow from serving six new clients per month to serving twelve to fifteen new people per month. Bill was already set up with an intake and engagement process that was bringing at least 80 percent of the people he engaged with at networking events. He was ready to take proactive control and engage in paid marketing. So, Bill licensed postcards from the *New Law Business Model* and sent them to 5,000 families in his community every six weeks. This resulted in a consistent supply of new clients every month. It worked so well that Bill is still marketing through direct mail today. It costs him about $5,000 or so every six weeks to run his campaign, but he's happy to make that investment in order to be in full control of his marketing. He doesn't have to wait for a corporation to invite him to speak, or do any networking at all.

LEVERAGE RESOURCES AND TRACK YOUR RESULTS

Whenever possible, seek to leverage the proven resources that have been created by the *New Law Business Model*. The danger with trying to create a similar plan yourself is that your content may sound like it was written by a traditional lawyer. By the same token, if you hire a marketing consultant to create the content for you, the writer will undoubtedly not understand your practice or your market and will have no experience in what works.

However, there is a need for content in other legal practice areas. For instance, if you're a lawyer who serves in immigration, bankruptcy, divorce, or real estate, and you have high quality content already created that you would like to leverage, feel free to contact my team to discuss how we can work with you to make that happen.

Whatever kind of marketing content you use, whether it's mailers, TV ads, radio ads, or presentations, you will want to drive people to a URL that's specific to the marketing touch, so you can track the response rate.

SHOULD YOU USE LEAD GENERATION SERVICES?

Many lawyers struggle with educating their communities. They don't want to practice estate planning or small business planning (so they can't use my content) and they don't know how to create their own. If you are one of these lawyers, one solution is to buy leads from online lead generation services, but with the caveat that before you do, you must know how to get hired and paid by these leads. Otherwise, it's a waste of your time and money.

For certain practice areas, such as immigration, bankruptcy, divorce, and personal injury, buying leads can work for you. People searching for a lawyer in these specialties are looking to hire someone right away, and they do not necessarily need to be educated as to why they need a lawyer. If you choose to buy leads in one of these practice areas, be prepared to handle them in a way that immediately establishes trust and differentiates you from the other lawyers they're calling while they shop around.

An immigration lawyer I know was losing 80 percent of the people who contacted his office and he didn't know why. He asked me to call his office, posing as a potential client, and then give him feedback on my experience. I did, and the problem was immediately clear: his intake process was awful. He was wasting a lot of money paying for leads that would never hire him because of how his phones were being handled. Training your intake team to follow a process that builds immediate trust is one of the highest return investments you can make.

I worked with a divorce lawyer in Canada to create a simple intake script and process that doubled his engagement rate from a dismal 25 percent to 50 percent. What we shifted is that as soon as someone emailed in, the client intake rep immediately got the prospective client on the phone to discuss options for booking the initial appointment. Then, we gave that initial appointment a name, a purpose, and a value. Even though the prospect would be getting the session for free, it was only because they agreed to do some homework ahead of time—and back their commitment to do that homework with a credit card.

By implementing this system, prospects came to their meeting prepared to hire the firm, having already done the pre-work necessary to be able to make a hiring decision. And, they kept their appointments because they were already invested in the process.

In areas like estate planning and business planning, online lead generation services are usually not so effective. People who need these types of legal services are not generally in a rush to hire a lawyer, as they are in other practice areas.

If you plan to use an online lead generation service for this kind of practice, you'll want to make sure you know exactly how to address the question of "how much does it cost" in a way that shifts the conversation from a specific set of documents your prospect thinks they need, and into a conversation around discovery of what they really need.

Also, you'll want to make sure that your leads come to you properly educated. For example, my company's website KidsProtectionPlan.com lets parents create free legal documents naming legal guardians for their kids. Other lawyers might look down on this, but they are stuck in a limited view, perhaps comparing the site to the many online legal document sites. In fact, the goal is to acknowledge that every adult needs legal documents, and then to separate legal documents from advice and education. We educate people on the fact that signed legal documents don't necessarily lead to effective outcomes, and then direct the ones who want those effective outcomes to the lawyers we've trained.

This type of online lead generation acts as a filter to proactively vet for clients who actually need our lawyers' services. Using education to filter your prospects is critical to protect your time, otherwise you could be wasting significant resources talking to people who aren't really ready for you.

A LAST WORD ON OMNIPRESENCE

Being omnipresent in your community means that the right clients see and hear about you everywhere—in their mailbox, in their email inbox, in their social media, in conversations with their friends and family, and at community speaking events. This doesn't happen overnight. You create it through intentional networking, educating your referral sources, using your speaking events wisely, and leveraging the support of your automation systems.

When you put all these pieces together, which can take up to three years, depending on how fast you invest in systems, it will happen for you.

By being willing to do what other lawyers won't, you differentiate yourself, not just by what you say, but by how you show up and are seen in your community. It doesn't have to be difficult, it just has to be intentional.

CHAPTER EIGHT

THE FIFTH SHIFT: EMBRACE MENTORSHIP

The fifth shift, embracing mentorship, allowed me to go from being a lawyer working for someone else in a BigLaw firm, to running my own practice and ultimately, building what I learned in my own practice into a multimillion-dollar business.

Unfortunately, along the way, I stopped seeking mentorship at various points, and when I did, I was not able to find my way through the breakdown points I hit without hitting rock bottom. Some people (like me, perhaps) do have to learn everything the hard way, but if possible you should always seek to leverage the wisdom of others who have gone before you, and build on what they've already learned. There really is no need to reinvent the wheel, in most cases.

WHAT IS A MENTOR?

Working with someone who has already done what you want to do allows you to leverage their knowledge and experience, so you don't have to reinvent the wheel. Like becoming omnipresent, benefiting from mentorship requires some mental microshifts.

First, to benefit from mentoring, you must be a willing student—a person who's open to learning from the wisdom of others. Then, you must find a teacher who's already done what you want to do, and is willing to take your hand and show you what they learned.

Benefitting from a mentor or mentorship program takes more than simply learning from their experience and teachings, though. Change—any change, not just the change you need to make to successfully adopt or transition to the *New Law Business Model*—requires more than that.

You can know (or be told) everything that's necessary to succeed, and yet still fail. Why does that happen? And, what's important for you to know about failure itself?

How can you know everything there is to do and still not do it?

The reason is that on the pathway to change, you will get stuck. You'll be afraid to take the next step. But for change to happen, you have to be supported to fail, move forward, and not only accept the possibility of failing again, but even look forward to it.

Failure is where you learn and grow.

Failure is a critical part of your learning process. And any good mentor should be helping you to fail fast, learn the right lessons from the failure, and move forward toward success.

Remember in chapter four, when I told you, "*If all you had to do was read a book to experience success, then every diet book, every fitness guide, and every self-help book out there would miraculously impart life-changing wonders on any reader who took the time to plow through its chapters.*" It's the same with mentoring. There is more to it than knowledge transfer. In the best mentoring situations, the mentorship you receive will keep you moving forward when you would otherwise quit.

Think of it in the context of working with a personal trainer. For example, if I'm left to my own devices, I would never work out. If I did manage to haul myself into the gym, I would never push my body to failure. On the other hand, when I work out with my personal trainer, I do the workout that I would never do on my own.

If my trainer tells me to do "mountain climbers" (which, if

you have never done them, are killer exercises that work your whole body) for a full minute, I do them—even if my mind and body is screaming at me to stop. If, after a minute, when I'm at the point of breakdown, my trainer says to keep going for another thirty seconds, I keep going. After all, if the trainer thinks I can do it, maybe I can! Just when I'm reaching my point of failure, thinking, I can't do one more second, he tacks on another ten seconds. That's when my mind shifts from I *can't* to I *can*, and I *do*. I push past the point of failure and that's where the transformation of my body (and mind) happens.

It's the same when you are building a business. You almost always find your transformation the moment everything falls into place, right when you are about to give up.

We see it a lot in our programs. Take Amy, for example. She'd been with us for a few years as a Personal Family Lawyer, doing pretty well, seeing four to six new clients a month, but she wanted to go to the next level and hire a support team, so she could increase her income and work less.

Hiring is always scary. And just when Amy brought on her first team member, her client engagements started to tank. Up until then, she had been consistently engaging just about everyone she met with. Then, all of a sudden, right after taking on a commitment to hire a client services director (CSD) and pay payroll each month, half of the people she met with didn't hire her. And then it got worse, and the next three people she met with didn't hire her, either.

Fortunately, Amy had a personal coach as part of her Personal Family Lawyer membership, and this coach helped Amy to see and understand what was happening. Without the coaching she received, Amy would have almost certainly fired her client services director and slipped backward into a lack of confidence and self-doubt about her ability to grow.

Instead, Amy's coach helped her to see that she had dropped parts of the *New Law* system when she brought her CSD on board. They returned to the trainings and videos and trained her CSD to do the same. Shortly after that, Amy was back to engaging 100 percent of the clients she met with, and at an even higher average engagement fee than before. Now, with support to serve her growing clientele, she can continue to grow.

This is where mentoring really happens: in the breakdown moments.

A mentor helps you make the change you desire, even when you can't see how it's possible.

To initiate change, you must first change your mindset about what's possible. You have to change the quality of your thinking and ideas. Being around people who are already doing what you want to do, who have already achieved that success, creates an environment conducive to change.

I wouldn't have done anything if I hadn't seen other people do it. That's why one of my mantras throughout building my business has been, "If she can do it, I can do it." Seeing people doing what I wanted to do changed my perspective on what was possible. And telling myself, again and again, "If he can do it, I can do it. If she can do it, I can do it" has never failed to change my mindset—my beliefs—on what is possible.

Work with a mentor who will encourage you to dream bigger than you ever have for yourself and support the actions you need to make big, necessary changes, and I promise, you'll see results. If you continue to do things the same way you've always done, you will have the same results you've always had. Those results aren't working for you—if they were, you wouldn't be reading this book.

Over the years, I have personally invested more than $250,000 in mentorship. As a result of that, my company generates that much (and often more) in one month. So, do mentors pay for themselves? Absolutely. If they're the right mentor, they've done what you want to do and have a bigger idea of what's possible for you than you might have for yourself. They believe in you more than you believe in yourself because they've moved through the failure and achieved the success you're looking for. They know how to make it a reality. A mentor takes you beyond your own capacity—beyond your breaking point and through the failure to success. Mentors help make change possible.

One of the biggest pitfalls I see is lawyers looking for free mentorship. If you are on Facebook groups or email list-servs, trying to obtain mentorship for free, stop it. It's simply leaving you spinning your wheels, wasting time and energy and going nowhere. Stop doing that. Invest in the right mentorship, and achieve your goals.

FIND THE RIGHT MENTOR

It can be very easy to hire the wrong mentor, because there's a lot of people out there selling mentorship who are great salespeople, but not great mentors. I learned this lesson the hard way, far too often hiring people who I *thought* could help me because they were really great at selling themselves, but really couldn't because they had not already done what I wanted to do. In some cases, they left me worse off than before I had hired them.

My first coach for my law practice helped me to believe that I could leave the BigLaw job and start my own practice, and I did it. But then, because of his own limited experience in business, he was not able to support me to build my law practice into the business I really wanted. Each time I shared an idea, vision, or dream with him, he shot it down as not possible. If I had listened to him, I'd probably still have a little law practice, around the size of his business, that would have kept me working nights and weekends and not really delivering a service I believed in. The traditional law practice model was his norm. But I wanted to create so much more than that.

Fortunately, I was able to quickly see that this mentor would not be able to support me to go where I wanted to go, and I ended the relationship, appreciating what I did receive (the courage to leave the BigLaw firm). I was then free to seek out the mentorship I would need to build the kind of practice I really wanted.

I had to look outside the legal industry to find mentorship that would truly support me, because back then no one had built the kind of law practice I sought to create for myself and my clients.

I ended up learning from carpet cleaners, magicians, dentists, chiropractors, and other professional service providers who were creating the kind of businesses that I envisioned for myself. I took the practices they had tested and proven in their industries and brought them over to my law practice.

Today, thanks to what I learned from these professional

service providers and tested in my own practice, I'm able to mentor lawyers to build next-level estate planning and strategic business counsel practices.

So, how do you know if someone is the right mentor for you? Look to whether they have already done what you want to do in your own life and law practice.

In the legal industry today there are many great mentors who did what I did—went outside the legal industry, learned to create a new model, and now help other lawyers to implement it.

Lee Rosen has done this in the field of divorce.

Ben Glass has done this in the field of personal injury.

Michael Rozbruch is doing it for CPAs and EAs.

If you can find a lawyer—ideally in your practice area—who has already done what you want to do in your life and law practice, learn all you can from them; use their proven and tested strategies, marketing materials, and systems. You will get to the success you want much more quickly than if you try to go it alone.

I maintain a list of lawyers providing mentoring in specific practice areas at newlawbusinessmodel.com/resources, so check there to see if we have a resource for you in your practice area.

THE MAGIC OF A MENTOR

I want to share a story that is both entertaining and educational about a mentor I hired to help me take my business to the next level. It cost me $30,000 to work with him, but really it cost me nothing at all because I've made millions over the years as a result of our work together. Millions I probably never would have gotten to on my own.

This is just one of many big investments I've made at each stage of my business growth, but this story is instructional for a few reasons. It illustrates for you how I chose to go all in, even when I didn't have the cash on hand to do it. I chose the right mentor and got magical results.

The story begins in the first year my practice hit a million in revenue. I was ready to expand beyond serving clients on a one-to-one basis and start teaching my methodologies to other lawyers and the families they serve.

Now, you might think that when you are bringing a million a year into your own law practice that you'll be on easy street with no cash flow issues, and the ability to invest in anything you want. But that's not true at all. Especially if, like me back then, you don't know how to manage the money coming in very well.

That million a year was going out as fast as I could bring it in. Especially because I had recently gotten divorced and had big legal bills in addition to having to split my savings with my husband, buy him out of his community property share of the practice, *and* pay child support and alimony.

So, while the practice was making a million a year, I really wanted to generate an additional $10,000 per month on top of my law firm income. I felt ready to leverage the things I had created in my own practice—like the Kids Protection Plan and my marketing and client engagement systems.

I found an event for people who had done what I wanted to do, and for people like me, who were on their way there. The catch? A week away from my kids and my business, plus $3,000 to attend the event in Cleveland, Ohio.

I did not make the decision to go lightly. It would be my first real time away from my kids, and I didn't have $3,000 in cash lying around after the divorce had drained my savings. Meeting mentors who could actually help me was a big decision—*huge*—because of the time and money it would cost, but by then I had figured out the critical importance of being around people who had done what I wanted to do, and I knew the investment was crucial to my next step.

This is where my story gets a little weird. I did end up meeting my mentor at the event, but he wasn't a lawyer. He wasn't even wearing a suit or carrying a briefcase. He did not look at all like what I expected a mentor to look like. Are you ready for this? He was a magician—a professional magician.

The first thing he asked me, "How much do you want to earn?" And that was the right question, because if he was going to take me on as a client, he had to evaluate whether he'd be able to help me reach my goals.

I had already given this number serious thought. Now divorced, I wanted to be able to pay my mortgage, my child support and my alimony, even if I never took on another client myself. "I want to earn an additional $10,000 a month," I answered. That, to me, would be *freedom*.

"No *problemo*," he said. Now, plenty of people would have said no problem, but I believed this guy because he had already done exactly what I wanted to do, and I could see that. He'd gone from being a magician booking three shows a month, and practically starving, to learning how to use his education-based marketing to book *fifty-seven shows a month*, which was way too many shows to do on his own. He then built a business teaching other magicians how to do what he'd done. And that's exactly what I wanted to do, though with lawyers and families, not magicians, of course.

I ended up hiring the magician at a $30,000 investment, and dipping into my credit line to do it. Crazy, right? Well, it felt crazy at the time. But, at the same time, I knew it would be a wise investment because if he could help me get to $10,000 a month in additional income, I could pay back that $30,000 in no time. I believed he would help me get there far faster than if I tried to do it on my own.

And he did.

In fact, the very first thing he did was help me focus in on the one thing that would get me where I wanted to go fastest. Prior to meeting him, my focus had been scattered, I'd been trying to do too many things at once. Because he had already been where I wanted to go, he was able to slow me down, laser my focus, and help me see that taking just one right step would lead to the big vision I was holding.

Within two months of working with my magician-mentor, I held my first training event, with 750 lawyers on a teleseminar. My biggest fear had been that I would only enroll one lawyer in my training. Instead, I ended up doing $117,000 in sales from that *one* call. Again, this was within *two months* of hiring my mentor. The experience totally changed my life. I did *exactly what he told me to do*—and I got exactly what I wanted. Within eighteen months, that first "teleseminar" I hosted would turn into my second million-dollar-a-year business, earning me far more than the additional $10,000 per month I'd been hoping to bring in.

A reminder: *when the student is ready, the teacher will appear.* And I was ready.

I knew exactly what my goals were: $10,000 per month. I trusted my mentor to help me laser focus on exactly what my next steps would be to get me to that big vision. I followed what he said exactly, learning his system before I tried to change any of it, and laid the foundation for my next level.

What's interesting for me to look back at is that today, this is the exact same process we use to help the lawyers we serve at *New Law Business Model*. We start by helping you get clear on your short-term goals and long-term vision, and then help you to laser in on exactly the next steps that will get you there, so you can focus instead of wasting energy being constantly scattered.

We've figured out that the first step for lawyers transitioning to the *New Law Business Model* is to learn the model by applying it to their own life and law practices first, by creating their own next-level estate plan for their family and putting in place their own LIFT (legal, insurance, financial and tax) systems. That way, no matter what, you get your own systems in place. And along the way, you make sure that you like the model you've chosen to work with. To use our systems, you'll need to learn our model, and get your own next-level estate plan in place.

Then, it's all about learning how to get hired by clients the way we teach. It doesn't make sense to do any marketing at all until you know how to get hired by every client you meet who needs your services. That's when marketing really pays off. Before you can do that, your marketing is often a waste of time and money.

But, once you know how to get hired by every client who needs your services, and at fees that pay you enough to deliver a great service, it makes sense to turn up the volume on your marketing. At the same time, you want to make sure you're doing the most efficient, effective marketing for the number of clients you can actually see and serve each month without going way over your capacity. That requires being able to look at your financial needs, plus the time you have available to meet those needs.

Once our mentees have learned the *New Law Business Model*, chosen the right practice model, and learned to engage clients, we license to them our proven, tested marketing content to help them become educators in their community.

If you're looking for your own next mentor (as I believe you should be), look for the following:

1. A mentor who has done what you want to do in their life and business, ideally using their law degree to create a high-value asset in the way you want to do.
2. A mentor who shares your values.
3. A mentor who truly believes in what's possible for you and even dreams bigger than you may for yourself.
4. A mentor whom you pay because you value their time, and they value their time.
5. A mentor who can significantly shortcut your learning curve and will help you take risks, fail fast, and learn the right lessons from your missteps.

You will go much farther, much faster, with the right mentor.

The five shifts you learned in these chapters aren't "nice-to-haves." In the *New Law Business Model*, they're *mandatory*. Every single one of our most successful lawyers made them, and they have lives and law practices they love as a result.

—

PART THREE

STARTING AND GROWING YOUR *NEW LAW BUSINESS MODEL* PRACTICE

CHAPTER NINE

HOW TO GET STARTED PRACTICING IN A NEW WAY

By now, you're clear and committed to making a change in your life and law practice. But where do you actually begin? Now it's time to dig deeper into creating the optimal *New Law Business Model* practice for you.

With that in mind, here are the steps to start:

CHOOSE YOUR PRACTICE AREA AND STOP BEING A DOOR LAWYER

The first step towards having a *New Law Business Model* practice is to focus on a single practice area in which you can become *the* go-to lawyer in your community for the legal services you provide.

That doesn't mean you need to provide legal services in this one practice area forever, but we do recommend you master one practice area first, with well-established systems for educating your community (becoming known as *the* expert due to your omnipresence strategy), and serving your clients in this one practice area until you have raving fans, before expanding to another area.

Many lawyers mistakenly think they need to take whatever business walks in the door, just to keep the doors open. As I've said, we call this being a door lawyer, and it's the fastest path to unhappiness for most lawyers.

Being a door lawyer means you can never develop systems, you can never become known as the go-to lawyer for your practice area of expertise, and you can never command premium fees. Instead, with each new client, you are reinventing the wheel—a jack-of-all-trades, and master of none.

You don't need to hedge your bets and do both criminal law *and* family law in an effort to have both services in your repertoire in case the economy shifts. Instead, create an economy-proof practice that will be needed no matter what the economy does. Then, go all-in learning how to deliver a great service and creating the systems to do so, while becoming omnipresent (the go-to lawyer for your service), so even if the economy does change, you're still the lawyer that gets hired for the services you provide. Great lawyers are always in demand. Again, become a great lawyer in *one* practice area.

Focusing on more than one practice area is a major pitfall most lawyers make in the beginning. And it's just scarcity thinking that causes you to do it, the belief that there aren't enough clients to go around in your practice area. But of course, there are. It's likely you need to learn marketing to reach those clients, but that's far easier to do when you only have *one* practice area to focus on.

Once you are consistently hitting your goals with the foundational success systems in place for attracting and engaging clients, serving them with "raving fan" client service systems, and managing your financials and your team, then, sure, add another complementary practice area. Just don't make that add until you have your first area *fully dialed-in.*

Then, if you're going to add another practice area, add a complementary service for the same clients that you serve in your primary practice. By doing that, you don't have to expand your marketing reach to a whole new audience, but can leverage the audience you've already built and provide additional services they want and need. Build on the relationship you've already created, rather than starting from scratch, again.

For example, I began with an estate planning practice,

serving young families in my community. Then, once I had established systems and was known as the go-to lawyer in my community for families, I began to educate business owners. This group was complementary because they needed estate planning, too. Once I had built my own businesses, and truly understood all that it takes to build a business from scratch and maintain success, I began to work with other business owners as a strategic advisor. Some of those business owners I had already served with estate planning.

It's all complementary. I just kept building upon what I had already created, expanding my offerings and reach, systematically.

Having said that, I do want to acknowledge that taking the first step and narrowing my focus to marketing *only* to families with young children in my community was terrifying and took me over a year to do, even after I had learned from Michael Port (author of *Book Yourself Solid)* that it was critical to focus on *one* market in order to get booked solid with clients. I'll talk more about how I overcame my fear of marketing to a narrow audience in the next section.

Your first step is to identify which practice area is going to best help you create a life and law practice you love.

How do you identify the best practice area for you, if

you haven't chosen yet? Well, you know we think estate planning and business planning are the best, but we also know that's not for everyone. So, we've created a quiz to support you to choose the right practice area and practice model for you! You can take the quiz at http://www. NewLawBusinessQuiz.com.

IDENTIFY YOUR IDEAL CLIENTS, WHERE TO REACH THEM AND HOW YOU WANT TO SERVE THEM

Once you've chosen the practice area that you want to serve, your next step is to identify the ideal clients you want to serve.

Now, I want to be very clear here that just because you identify the ideal clients you want to serve, this does not mean you will not serve other clients who come into your office and do not match this demographic.

You identify the ideal clients you want to serve so that you can narrow and focus your marketing systems and become omnipresent to a small group of people.

I see too many lawyers I teach about this get confused here, so I want to be very, very clear. You focus your marketing to reach and educate your ideal clients about your services. For example, I focused my marketing on educating young families in my community about the need for estate planning that would ensure their kids were never taken into the care of strangers, or raised by anyone they wouldn't want. But, when I did that, all of a sudden I was getting more calls than ever from people who didn't have minor children, like wealthy grandparents and business owners. When that happened, if the people calling me didn't have minor children but I could serve them with my expertise, I of course did. I didn't turn them away as long as it was clear that they needed my services.

When you focus your marketing on just reaching your ideal client, it brings in all sorts of people who are attracted to your expertise and focus, whether or not they fall directly into the bucket of people you've identified as your ideal client for marketing purposes.

Your ideal clients are the people who you truly want to make a difference for with your services, who you enjoy spending time with, and who you will build your law practice systems to serve.

In my case, when my children were little, I chose to serve families with young children because that's the stage of life I was in, and I was surrounded by parents with young kids. I knew the people who needed my services, where they spent their time, the magazines they read, the events they attended, what kept them up at night, and how to speak to them in a meaningful way.

Later on, when I began to think of myself as a real business owner, I started to serve business owners.

One of the best parts of having a law degree and serving people who are already part of your community is that you get the satisfaction of knowing that you are using your law degree to help the people you care about.

Start looking around your community now to identify who needs your services the most, that you will love to spend your time educating.

Go back to your journal and describe this person in detail.

One of the exercises we have our members in training do when they first join us is to make a list of all the people they already know who need estate planning services. Then, we teach them to get curious with the people in their community about their past experiences with estate planning, using what we call "curiosity questions," in which the lawyer asks the people they already know if they've ever done estate planning, and if so, what their experience was like. If not, they ask, "Why not?"

If you were to do this, you'd likely find that most people have a personal story in their own family of a situation in which faulty estate planning caused conflict or mired the family in a long-drawn-out court process. You would likely also find that most people want to keep their family out of court and conflict. If that's the case, you may want to consider that estate planning could be a great practice area for you to consider, and that learning to do it in a way that is truly impactful could be a great next step for you.

PRICE AND PACKAGE YOUR SERVICES USING THE *NEW LAW BUSINESS MODEL* PRINCIPLES

Once you've got your practice area dialed in, and you've identified who you want to serve, you can price and package your services to meet the needs of your ideal clients.

This does *not* mean that you should create a retainer system that has you billing hours against a retainer. Nor does it mean that you should be billing low flat fees, like $99 for unlimited access to you on a subscription program. None of this works!

Instead, use your Money Map to create package options that deliver your service in a way that works for you and your clients. Align your interests with getting paid well for a great service with your clients' interests to receive a high-value outcome that they want and need.

Then, create a fee schedule that illustrates your packages, so that your clients can choose their own fee when working with you, based on their needs and desires and the level of service that's right for them.

If you'd like to see the packages we've created for families and small business owners as a model for what you can create, check out our service offerings at newlawbusinessmodel.com/resources.

CREATE AN INTAKE AND ENROLLMENT STRUCTURE THAT PROPERLY PREPARES YOUR CLIENTS TO HIRE YOU

Intake and enrollment is the lifeblood of your law practice. If you're wasting time in initial consultations that *don't* result in your prospective clients hiring you on the spot, you're going to burn out, or worse, go out of business.

Fixing your intake and enrollment structure pays off in spades because it not only saves you time, but it makes you money. And when you know you can get hired by every person you meet with who needs your services at average fees that pay you well to deliver a great service, a lot of things shift in your practice for the better.

Suddenly, you have confidence that you can pay for support, instead of having to do it all alone. *Now* it starts to make sense to invest in marketing.

But until you have an intake and enrollment structure that gets you hired by everyone who needs your services, you'll often feel frustrated that your networking doesn't work or your marketing isn't paying off. It's the worst of the worst.

So, fix your intake and enrollment structure. I put together a five-step report to get you started at newlawbusinessmodel. com/resources.

BUILD AND TRAIN THE RIGHT-SIZE TEAM FOR YOUR PRACTICE MODEL

Even if you're a *Solo Practitioner*, you'll still need some help. It doesn't make sense for you, with your law degree and valuable expertise, to be doing tasks that you can easily outsource. Your goal is to build and train your team—whether that's one assistant and some outsourced folks or a fully staffed office—so you can focus on educating your community and engaging clients.

And the size of your team should match the number of clients you want and need to serve to hit your personal, financial, and time goals.

I often find that when I'm working with lawyers (or any business owners for that matter) on growing their businesses, there's a pendulum swing back and forth between a focus on sales and marketing and getting enough clients in the door and ensuring you have the capacity to serve those clients.

When this happens intentionally and strategically, it's a lot less crazy-making for you as the business owner.

So, the way I like to see it go is as follows:

STAGE ONE: IDENTIFY YOUR FIRST-STAGE INCOME MODEL

- In this stage, you're serving all the clients on your own. Get real about how many clients you can serve each month without hiring any support, as it's probably fewer than you think.
- Focus your first-level sales and marketing efforts on enrolling just that many clients with a priority on getting yourself to a near 100 percent engagement rate. With a near 100 percent engagement rate of everyone who needs your services, and at fees that are high enough for you to deliver a great service, you can feel confident that you can hire support.*
- Once you've hit that first-level goal and are at capacity (meaning you cannot serve any additional clients with

---

* While a 100% engagement rate, or anything close to it, may sound crazy to you, it's actually a critical component of having a law practice you love. And it's totally possible as it's the case for the lawyers who follow our New Law Business Model education, intake, and engagement systems for getting hired by families and small business owners. Think about it this way: if you properly educate your prospects, and they come through a well-designed intake structure, complete homework ahead of time, and then meet with you for an educational session that helps them choose HOW to work with you, why wouldn't they hire you? You've just made it extremely easy for them to do what they know they want and need to do, and you're helping them choose the best way to work with you. So if you don't think a 100% engagement rate is possible, it could just be that you don't really understand what your prospects want and need, or how to help them choose it. Or it may be that you don't have a client engagement system well-constructed to lead to engagement nearly 100% of the time. Start tracking how much time you are spending with people who don't hire you, or who hire you at too low of a flat fee or on an hourly billing model that isn't good for you or your clients, and see what it's really costing you to not have a great client engagement system in place.

ease), and you know you can engage just about everyone you are meeting with, go to the next level.

STAGE TWO: DOUBLE YOUR CAPACITY

- First things first: hire a client services director. Your CSD is your partner in expanding your capacity to serve more clients. (I mean partner in relationship terms, not in name, because we know that non-lawyers can't own law firms.)
- Hire a bookkeeper. Do not attempt to do your bookkeeping on your own. It's not a good use of your time, and you want to start getting used to someone else handling your books for you and giving you the reports you'll need to start to run your law practice as a business.
- Note that by hiring and training the *right* client services director and starting to work with a bookkeeper, you will likely double your capacity from your stage one income model. But once your CSD is trained and your bookkeeper is doing their job well, you'll be working less *and* bringing in twice the revenue. And these two additional team members will cost you far less than that additional revenue, which means you keep more money too.
- The key here, of course, is knowing you can double the number of appointments you've got on the calendar, and with the right marketing strategies and systems, you can!

- Start to build in a routine of weekly marketing meetings with yourself and your CSD, a weekly review of metrics with your CSD, a weekly financial review with yourself, and a monthly meeting with your bookkeeper to go over the P&L (profit and loss) to make sure income and expenses are properly categorized.

STAGE THREE: TRIPLE YOUR CAPACITY

- Once you've doubled your capacity with just your client services director, it's time to get support to expand your marketing and triple your capacity. That could look like mastering educational presentations and running direct mail campaigns to fill them. Yes, this requires investment, but if you know how to do presentations that convert, and you know that everyone you meet with who needs your services hires you, there's very little risk and very high reward.
- Hire an outreach-intake coordinator. This person's role is to do outreach in your community to get you speaking, to follow up on all presentations and networking events to intake new prospects, and to ensure that every prospect comes in ready to hire you (thanks to your already created and proven intake process and enrollment structure).
- With one more hire here (likely an assistant to your client services director, or a file clerk/receptionist), you'll be able to get to a model in which you work part

time (three-and-a-half days a week) and keep your practice full and happily serving your clients. Hello, *Staffed Practice*!

STAGE FOUR: CONSIDER BRINGING ON OTHER LAWYERS

- Once you've mastered your intake and enrollment systems and have a great team supporting you to handle your outreach and client service, you may be ready to bring on one or more counsel attorneys, training them on your engagement process and expanding your capacity to serve more clients—without having to see them all, yourself.
- Now you have the capacity for a seven-figure practice, and since you aren't the only lawyer in the office engaging clients, you can start to look at a reality where you can take two to four weeks out of the office at a time. Hello, *7-Figure Firm Owner*!

Making the investments to move through these stages is usually the scary part about building a life and law practice you love. And you don't need to move through all of these stages. **You can stop at any of the stages.** What you *don't* want to do is get stuck in between, because that's the worst place to be. So, choose where you want to go, and then go all-in to get there. And, get the support you need to keep going when you want to quit. Because you WILL want to quit at various points along the way. That's normal. And one of the key differentiators between success and failure is whether you have the support you need to keep going in those moments.

To watch a training I held on how to know which investments to make at which stage, and to properly set your goals based on where you are now and where you want to go next, go to newlawbusinessmodel.com/resources and watch the training on investing to grow your practice from one stage to the next.

CREATE A RAVING FAN SERVICE EXPERIENCE FOR YOUR IDEAL CLIENTS

One of the best parts about identifying an ideal client to serve is that you can create a raving-fan client experience. That's the kind where your clients tell everyone they know about their great experience with you. This kind of word of mouth marketing is the highest impact, least expensive marketing you can possibly have, and it comes as a result of how you treat the clients who hire you *after* they've paid you.

This is where you can truly create impact. Most lawyers collect payment and essentially vanish, leaving their client filled with uncertainty about what should happen next.

Remembering that most people are scared of lawyers (yes, even you, even though you are one of the good ones), it's always worthwhile to go out of your way to create an experience in which people feel safe with you. That's what will have clients walking out of your office saying "Wow, I never expected to have that kind of an experience with a lawyer." And they'll tell everyone they know about you.

Using *the New Law Business Model* systems, after twenty-five years of practicing the old way, Steven O'Neill wrote to tell us:

> "At the end of the meeting, [my clients] were saying things like, 'We really loved filling out the questionnaire, and 'We're thankful that you've taken us through this process,' and 'This is the best thing we've ever done.' I have to tell you, I've been doing this for thirty years, and I'd never had anyone say that."

You can bet that those clients went and told their kids, and their parents, and their friends that they needed to work with Steven.

Because our lawyers have implemented a raving fan service from the moment of their first contact with a prospect via email or phone to the time that the client has a plan in hand, and a meeting with their family introducing their lawyer, our lawyers consistently report that their clients pay them not just financially, but with massive appreciation in the form of gifts, referrals, and testimonials.

When you have a specific practice area, and build your practice to serve the needs of a specific demographic, you can create this kind of a raving fan service, and it pays off in spades.

CHAPTER TEN

GROWING YOURSELF AS YOU GROW YOUR PRACTICE

As you grow your practice, you will need to grow yourself along the way. Moving from stage to stage in your practice requires you to become the person who has the capacity to show up and hold more at each stage. To fuel this external growth, you also need internal growth.

When I speak about showing up and holding more at each stage, you may not know what that means—when I first started out, I probably wouldn't have. So, I want to make it really clear for you.

Showing up and holding more means that as you move from solo practitioner to hiring your first team member to leading a whole staff, and maybe even training other attorneys, you have to become a more mature person.

At each of these steps, you also need to learn to make bigger and bigger investments in the practice, which takes something, too.

Remember, when you have a million-dollar-a-year practice, you're writing checks or paying bills each month in the neighborhood of $60,000 or more before a single dollar comes to you.

My guess is that you've never had the experience of moving so much money through your bank accounts, and as you can imagine, this can be quite scary at first.

The way I handled my fear was not very good.

Mostly, I found myself grouchy, ungrateful, demanding, and perfectionistic. And that's when things were going well!

I'm sort of kidding, but also not.

I had learned leadership from my dad (who had a lot of charisma, but limited leadership skills) and the law firm partners at that BigLaw firm, some of whom were really great, but others who were stuck in patterns I'm sure we all know well.

Leadership is a trait we hear a lot about, but we don't necessarily have the best models for in our own lives.

So, yes, grouchy, ungrateful, demanding and perfectionistic was my leadership style. And, at the same time, I thought I was the best boss ever because I didn't have a lot of structure for my employees, and let them pretty much come and go as they pleased, so long as they were getting the job done.

Turns out that's not actually what employees want.

Employees want structure, routine, clear metrics of success, regular reviews to know how they are doing, and to feel as if they are part of a winning team.

That requires you to become a person who can provide all of that, and to let go of any parts of yourself that feel as if you are superior because you went to law school. You need to let go of the part of you that believes your employees should be grateful just because you're signing their paychecks. You need to become a person who can set clear metrics of success, communicate them clearly, and manage your emotions when things are getting scary financially.

Now, listen, I didn't know any of this when I was starting out in business. In fact, it's probably the piece of the business puzzle that took me the longest to learn. I don't think I fully came to understand the meaning of leadership until just a couple of years ago.

In fact, when I sold my law practice, I didn't realize how important leadership was, which was why I sold it to a guy who had never run a million-dollar-law practice, never led a team, or even had any employees at all. No wonder I was surprised when within six months, he handed the law practice back to me and said he couldn't run it; I could either take it back or he would close it down.

That was my first lesson in learning that being a million-dollar-practice owner is not just about perfecting the systems, it's about who you become in the process of growing the practice. And, that's a huge part of what we help you with at the *New Law Business Model*, which I think really sets us apart from other training companies.

We support you to become a leader in your life, law practice and community.

If I had to define leadership in a way that most people would be able to understand it, I think I would say it's the ability to see the big picture, set a clear directional compass to get there, and then manage your emotions and stay calm and focused and in appreciation, even when the shit's hitting the fan along the journey.

Unless you've built a successful, sustainable, and thriving business before or been an executive in a company, you probably have little or no experience with any of this. You haven't been taught to find, hire, and train teams. You haven't learned how to manage your emotions when you're scared. Perhaps you've picked up leadership ideas from other lawyers—including the flaws I saw in myself and many lawyers around me.

We lawyers can be impatient and intimidating. We tend to have some degree of a superiority complex, while at the same time we may feel deeply insecure. Some of us (raising my hand here) went to law school to prove that we were good enough, or that we were smart enough. We went because we like to be in control.

None of this is conducive to leading people to do their best. To build a great team, you must be a great leader. Fortunately, just like math, leadership *is* a skill you can learn. If I did it, you can too.

Lawyers who work with my team and me receive a lot of guidance on how to grow into the leaders they need to be, so they can hire the right people, inspire them, and create practices they are proud of.

BE THE LEADER

As you grow through the stages of your practice growth, you will learn to be the leader your team, your family, and your community needs you to be. Your law practice is the perfect practice space for you to learn to do this, and your job is to keep seeing the opportunities for growth as they arise.

You get to learn to provide clear expectations, boundaries, and structure. Your team wants it. You also get to learn to take full responsibility for when things don't work and change course without blame, shame, or judgment of yourself or your team.

As the leader, you get to be aware of times when your own frustration is causing a problem, and you get to be able to identify the source of your frustrations. Instead of blaming the outside world, the economy, your team, or your clients, you get to see that when something isn't working, there is always a solution. As the leader, you get to be committed to solutions-oriented thinking and getting out of the way, so your team can do what you hired them to do.

On that note, it's important you know exactly what you're hiring someone to do. You need to have systems in place for your team members to use, and to train them on those systems. Here's a simple example: if you hire someone to answer your phone, you have to educate them to answer the phone the way you want it answered, not the way they answered it in a previous position. For example, you should have a particular greeting established (for ideas, check out our sample intake and initial consultation reports at newlawbusinessmodel.com/resources). Train your team member to answer your phone as you've delineated, then give them clear feedback on how they're doing.

MANAGING YOUR PEOPLE AND YOURSELF

While you want to be clear in your expectations, micromanaging your team is not a recipe for success. Set clear expectations around your goals, and what the practice needs to succeed. Then provide the systems to meet those goals, while allowing your team the space to make mistakes and course-correct each step of the way.

Making mistakes is part of the learning process. You will need to get good with allowing yourself to make mistakes before you'll be comfortable allowing your team members the same freedom.

Here's what that might look like: You've just hired your client services director to increase your capacity from serving four clients a month to eight clients a month. You need to do that within three months to hit your personal, financial, and time goals, and to be able to continue to pay your CSD her $5,000 a month salary.

When your CSD starts, you give her the big picture, ninety-day objective: to serve eight new clients a month. You give her the training resources she will need to handle intake of new prospects, prepare them for their initial meeting with you, and then serve them after they've engaged you. You set timelines for her learning, and then weekly meetings to review her progress, evaluate what's working and what's not, and find out what additional support resources she needs.

Within two weeks, she starts handling her first intakes, and by the third week you have the results of her first set of intakes to review together. You identify what worked, and what didn't, so she can learn from her mistakes. While you are able to see that she lost some folks that could have turned into clients, you aren't angry or frustrated by that, but instead see that it's part of the learning experience, and the more noes she gets and reviews with you, the closer she is to getting to yes with each prospect she talks with.

If, at that first review meeting, you discover that she is not coachable, not taking responsibility for her learning, and seems unwilling to see where the mistakes are and up-level, you let her go quickly and find someone else. This is the most important role in your office, and having the right person in this seat is the key to your next level of growth.

Managing your team begins with managing yourself. You

are learning how to lead, and humility goes a long way. If you are someone with a strong inner critic, or with control or perfection issues, you have to be careful about not projecting those onto your employees. If you think that you're smarter because you have a law degree, remember that there are different kinds of intelligence out there. You hire people to do work better than you can for yourself, and if they're the right people for the job they should be respected for their skills and talents.

Don't expect them to read your mind and then get frustrated when they can't. Practice outcome-based management, not task-based management, which is basically micro-management. Everyone hates to be micromanaged; it's disempowering. Don't tell your file clerks how to do their job, task-wise. Instead, tell them the outcome you want, the resources available, and check in with them once a week to see whether or not they're achieving their outcomes, and how you can support them if they are not.

This is another reason knowing your numbers and maintaining financial metrics is so critical. When you and your team are all on the same page, you are all striving to reach the same goals and reaching them. Your team will need to rely on the systems you've put in place, and you will need to train them on those systems.

Finally, your team should have a clear picture of how their

work contributes to the overall success of your practice, and the impact they have on your clients' lives and on your community. People want to be a part of something bigger than themselves, and when you can help them see their roles and contributions in your business, they will invest in what you do. They will stay with you for the long haul, becoming a loyal, dependable team that loves what they do as much as you do.

SYSTEMS? WHAT SYSTEMS?

You've heard me talk a lot about systems in this book. And, you may be wondering what systems I'm talking about, given that your practice has been running pretty much without any systems thus far.

So let's begin by defining systems for these purposes. System: a repeatable, replicable process for achieving your objectives.

As you grow your practice, you will need systems for attracting clients, getting hired by those clients, serving those clients, turning them into raving fans, and then ideally keeping them for life. Those are the outward-facing systems. Then, you'll also need inward-facing systems for managing your team, your metrics, your time, and your financials.

Given where technology is today, ideally you will automate

many of those systems. Back when I started in my practice, I had to use Excel spreadsheets and manual checklists for most everything I systematized.

Today, though, technology can automate almost all of your systems. It does require financial investment and time to set up your automation systems, but the investment is well worth it because once created, they will serve you and your practice for many years to come.

Here's an example: with an automated client engagement system, as soon as you meet someone in the community who needs your services or who might be a referral source for you, you put that person into your automation system. Then your system can begin reaching out to them on an automated basis, with a new contact nurture sequence that informs your new prospect about who you are and how you can serve them, ideally dripped out to them over time.

At the *New Law Business Model,* we've created an automation system for our lawyers to use that does just that, as well as automate and systematize the process for intaking a new prospect who is ready for an initial meeting. Once the client is engaged, our system will then proactively communicate with the client through the whole process of working together. Finally, we've automated the process of maintaining a plan over time with reviews every three years. Our membership maintenance program generates recurring revenue for our lawyers while their clients' plans stay up to date year in and year out.

Ideally, if you have the money to invest, you will set up your automation systems before hiring your team, so that when they come on board they are getting trained on the systems they will use.

Alternatively, what you can do is bring on an initial team member, such as your CSD, while you still have your old manual systems in place. Once you are consistently hitting your revenue milestones, you and your CSD can work together to build out your automation systems.

HAVE THE LEADERSHIP TO INVEST IN YOUR BUSINESS

Without question, at least in my book, the most difficult part of growing into your leadership will be continuing to make the investments necessary to grow from one stage of practice to the next.

You've heard the saying "it takes money to make money," and it's true. The good news is that money truly is infinitely renewable when you know how to earn it. And when you've got a hugely valuable asset like a law degree, earning it is actually rather easy—as long as you keep focusing your time, energy, and attention in the right direction.

In the early days of my law practice, investing in the growth of my practice was extremely scary. I didn't know which investments were wise, and which were folly. But I came to see clearly in this area, after many years of doing it very wrong, and making extremely expensive mistakes along the way.

Whenever I would get scared of the investments I was making, I would think of the dentists I knew who'd graduated dental school and then needed to invest in extremely expensive equipment and a big office and team to manage all of their patients. I would think of my dentist and how he made those investments knowing he had a service that people wanted and needed, and that he was able to make the hundreds of thousands of dollars of investments in his equipment, office and team because he knew that he'd pay those investments back many times over.

By doing that thought exercise, I'd be able to get out of the silly-but-common lawyer mindset that I shouldn't have to invest in technology, equipment, offices, or a team to have a thriving practice. I'd remind myself that I wanted to grow a business that would support the life I wanted, not one that would only let me be successful financially if I worked all hours of the day and night.

All successful businesses require upfront investments. The question to ask is what to invest in and when. Knowing the answer to that requires you to be clear on where you are now, where you want to go over the next three years, and what will need to happen in one year to get you there. Then, you can make the investments that will support your stage-by-stage growth.

I had no idea how to figure any of this out in the early years of my life in business. But since then, I've learned a whole lot. I've done it for myself, and also for you. If you'd like to see the three-year staged progression growth plan I've put together to help guide your investment decisions in your life and law practice, check out the cash flow forecasting through staged growth training at newlawbusinessmodel. com/resources.

CONCLUSION

LOVE YOUR PRACTICE, LOVE YOUR LIFE

I understand how hard it is to make a radical transition in your life and law practice, and I hope that this book and the work I've done at the *New Law Business Model* will make it as easy as possible for you.

You will undoubtedly encounter resistance along the way. Resistance will keep you from handling your time in the right way. You'll tell yourself things like, "Implementing time blocking on my calendar will restrict my freedom," and even try to convince yourself that making financial investments in your practice will put you out of business.

Resistance is normal when you are moving and growing outside your comfort zone. Recognize this resistance, but don't let it stop you. The way through resistance is to get a vision for your future that's bigger than the fear that's holding you back; your vision will pull you through the resistance and on to success.

There's a book called the *War of Art* by Steven Pressfield. It's written for writers, but it's useful for anyone who needs to see where that resistance comes from, so they can identify what it is that's keeping them from having what they want. If resistance is holding you back from building your law practice, I recommend that book.

The bottom line—whether you're a recent law school graduate, a lawyer working at a big firm, or a solo practitioner—is that you can have a life and law practice you love, with the fulfillment of knowing that going to law school was the right decision. You can absolutely be fulfilled being a lawyer and have total control of your money and time, when you learn to use your law degree in the *New Law Business Model* way.

Remember how I told you that one of my mantras all along has been *If she can do it, I can do it*? I wouldn't be living the life of my dreams had I not seen someone else do it first.

And if I can do it, you can do it, too.

RESOURCES

Know what you want to build. Go through the *Money Map for Lawyers* at moneymapforlawyers.com. It's free.

Then join our Facebook group for more support at newlawbusinessmodel.com/awesomelawyers.

Find all of the additional free resources we've referenced throughout the book, to support you to implement the *New Law Business Model* into your life and law practice at newlawbusinessmodel.com/resources.

ACKNOWLEDGMENTS

If anyone knows how important an acknowledgment section can be, it's me. It was by reading the acknowledgments in Robin Fisher Roffer's book that I found my first coach, Mariette Edwards. That's why my first acknowledgment is to those two women, who probably have no idea how much they're responsible for what I've created. Robin, thank you for showing me the first inkling of what a life and law practice built on freedom could look like. And Mariette, thank you for helping me learn how to take care of myself as the first step on the path to happiness.

My next set of acknowledgments is to a group of men who showed me what it looked like to love being a tax lawyer: Martin Ginsberg, Stephen Rose, Todd Molz, and Steven Guise. I had no idea I would love tax law so much, but you showed me the way. And you also helped me to see that I was not going to be able to survive at the BigLaw firm for life. You likely have no idea how much you impacted me with your friendship, but you did, significantly.

Next up are the lawyers who introduced me to the idea of estate planning far beyond the documents. Scott Farnsworth, you were way ahead of your time, and I am exceedingly grateful for the impact you've had on my life and my law practice—as well as on the lives and practices of all the lawyers I've been able to help, thanks to you. This applies to you as well, Rick Randall. Though we haven't yet (as of this writing) figured out how to work together, you've always been a light of possibility for me.

I never would have left BigLaw to start my own law firm had I not had the support of the upstart (at the time) document drafting software, WealthCounsel. It was a great confidence builder to know I had the best documents to support my services. And having Lew Dymond available to answer my many questions while I was trying to figure out how to serve my clients meant the world to me.

Diedre Wachbrit Braverman, seeing you, as a solo lawyer and a mom, build a successful, $25,000-a-month estate planning practice was the impetus for my first knowing "if she can do it, I can do it." So thank you for going first and supporting me to believe in myself.

Susan Odle, my first ever real team member, my client services director, and the woman for whom I created every one of the systems we used in our law practice, thank you for partnering with me to build Martin Neely & Associates into what it became, as quickly as it did. Neither one of us had any idea what we were doing, but we figured it out, together. And I truly cannot thank you enough for putting up with me at each step of the way. I'm glad we still get to work together, but that now you have a way better boss.

Speaking of which, Corey and Anna Whitaker, there are really no words that can properly express how grateful I am to you. I hope you know how thankful I am for your support in raising my kids, moving my houses, and handling my money through all the ups and downs over the years. Knowing you've had my back has meant everything.

Dave, I don't know that you will ever see this, but if you do, thank you for magically appearing in my life at just the right time. I'm sure I would have figured it out without you, but at what cost and how much time?

Craig, your work was not for nothing. The *New Law Business Model* is realizing its full potential. You were just a wee bit ahead of your time with it. I can never thank you enough for bringing Allison Osborn into my life and businesses. And Allison, I hope you know how very, very, very grateful I am to you for saying yes to me and to relational leadership. Thank you for being such a damn great human.

Speaking of relational leadership, I'm so grateful to you, Josh Zemel, for knowing that it would change my life and insisting that I get trained in it. It's thanks to you that we are now training lawyers to be relational lawyers. So, we all thank you! And of course, Josh Levin, thanks for saying yes to bringing relational leadership training to the lawyer community, and for creating the most important training we offer to our lawyer community with Allison and me.

I love and thank every single one of you lawyers who have said yes to relational training, and especially the first group of twelve who came out to Boulder with very little idea of what you were getting yourselves into: Irene, Hector, Alison, Stan, Rozita, Charles, Deb, Marianne, Matt, Corina, Bev, and Angela.

I want to acknowledge a group of people who supported the first iteration of what is now the *New Law Business Model*. LauraLee, Amber, Michelle, Chelsea, Dawn M, Dawn P, Melanie and Martha, you bore the brunt of my learning to become a good leader, and I'm in deep gratitude for the role you played in this work for lawyers.

Robert Kandell, LuAnne Hage, and Raj Sundra, I will always remember and be grateful for your push to say yes to the next level. I would not have done it without your encouragement and support. And with that encouragement and support, I was able to create a real lead team for the first time. I'm also thankful to Amy Jones and Theodore Tehrani for stepping into that team along with us and supporting me as I learned to lead. It makes me incredibly happy that we created a reality in which you are able to work with the *New Law Business Model* and pursue your passions at the same time.

Susanna Maida, Lindsay Chrisler, Scott DeStephanis, Jessica Seguin, Eric Scheele, Carrie Norton, Afi Harrington, Trevor Stevenson, Ariel RK, Monica DiCesare, Carly Karpovage, Lindsey Walker, Chris Towery, and Nicole Case, thank you for learning to serve our lawyers with so much care. We could not do what we do without you. Amber Manning, I am over the top grateful for your support in up-leveling our curriculum.

Jen, thank you for revamping our web presence to the next level. Ever grateful to see us through your eyes. We look so much better with your vision! And Amanda Steinberg, thanks for seeing me in general, and bringing Jen to us. Chrissie Bettencourt and Amanda Tarpening and Gretchen Lehman, your holding of our campaigns and communications with the outside world, while you parent your littles is *so* appreciated, and I'm so glad the *NLBM* is able to support you as you support us.

Bonnie and Tom Bowles, thank you for partnering with me on Accelerator, and putting your tech skills to use in support of the *New Law Business Model* way of educating lawyers and serving communities. Your "yes" to New Law Business Model and Accelerator makes so much more possible for our lawyer community. Infinite gratitude.

Andrew Thomaides, thank you for coming on as my partner to continue building the *New Law Business Model* into what it can be. Yay, I'm so glad you're here! Words aren't quite enough to express the gratitude, so I hope you can fully feel it. And for bringing Karl Becker to us. Karl, thank you for bringing your systematic thinking and self-awareness. It's such a great combination!

And, to you lawyers who have continuously inspired me to keep going, as early adopters of the *New Law Business Model* in your own lives and law practices, before the *NLBM* was even a thing: Darlynn Morgan, Nicole Newman, David Feakes, Denise Gosnell, Gerry Kane, Vanessa Terzian, Martha Hartney, and Robert Galliano. All of you, it's so good to see you living the dream.

And infinite gratitude to our current *Law Business* Mentors and Ambassadors: Yaasha Sabba, Don Gary, AJ Yolofsky, Irene DeJesus, Marc Garlett, Shane Young, Eileen Mastricht, and Jill Gregory! You are doing it and helping us serve more lawyers to do it too, and I'm so appreciative. Stan P., a special note of love and appreciation for you because I just know we're going to be serving lawyers together one day. :)

There is no way I'd have been able to write this book without the support I have at home. I'm amazed at how true it is that it takes a village. Thank you Kat and Georgia and Nena and Amber and Gili and Todd. And Will, thank you for seeing me and loving me and encouraging me to keep going. Amy and Mom and Courtney, your love and acceptance and support of me is what's made it all possible.

This book would never have gotten written without the support of Genevieve Field and the whole team at Scribe Media. So, thank you for your persistence and sticking with me. And, Mylee Blake, thank YOU for swooping in at the end to actually get this baby out the door with me.

Whew, that's a lot of people, and I'm quite sure it isn't even close to everyone! So if I've missed you, I'm sorry, please forgive me, thank you, I love you. And it just means that we need more connection before the next book is written, so reach out and let's reconnect.

ABOUT THE AUTHOR

ALI KATZ graduated first in her class, summa cum laude, from Georgetown University Law. Ali is still licensed under her former name Alexis Martin Neely in California, bar number 212365. She served a clerkship on the Eleventh Circuit Court of Appeals before joining one of the top law firms in the country, Munger, Tolles & Olson.

At twenty-nine, while co-parenting two very young children, Ali left her lucrative position at Munger, Tolles to launch her own law practice. Within three years, she had built that practice into a million-dollar-a-year-revenue-generating business, and went on to write the bestselling book on legal planning for families, *Wear Clean Underwear*, and appear on all the top television shows to educate families about it and the new practice methodology she had created for serving families with young children. Eventually, Ali created what is now the *New Law Business Model* to train other lawyers on how to attract, engage, and serve families and small business owners as a true Trusted Advisor.

Since creating this new way of practicing law, Ali has taught thousands of lawyers her methods and witnessed the extraordinary results when lawyers align their outcomes with those of their clients to build six- and seven-figure legal practices that have a positive impact on their communities, their clients, and their own lives.

Ali lives in Boulder, Colorado, where she and her ex-husband, Todd, co-parent their kids, Kaia and Noah.